T. S. Kuhn and Social Science

T. S. Kuhn and Social Science

Barry Barnes

Columbia University Press
New York   1982

Published in 1982 in the United States of America by
Columbia University Press

Library of Congress Cataloging in Publication Data

Barnes, Barry.
  T. S. Kuhn and social science.

  Bibliography: p.
  Includes index.
  1. Kuhn, Thomas S.   2. Science — Social
aspects. I. Title.
Q143.K83B37   303.4′83   81–38454
ISBN 0–231–05436–X   AACR2
ISBN 0–231–05437–8 (pbk)

Printed in Hong Kong

Say what you choose, so long as it does not prevent you from seeing the facts. (And when you see them there is a good deal that you will not say.)

Wittgenstein

It is a truism that anything is similar to, and also different from, anything else.

Kuhn

Contents

Preface

When I was invited to write this book I was immediately attracted by the importance of its subject, and by the pleasure I knew I should derive from working upon it. None the less I did have one initial reservation. Thomas Kuhn's work is widely known, readily intelligible and easily obtained. Its account of scientific research and the growth of knowledge is an accepted point of reference throughout the academic world. Hence I could find no excuse for something which simply expounded Kuhn's views, at a time when many areas of sociology are already so involved in the examination of seminal texts that they risk becoming backwaters of intellectual history.

Fortunately, however, the brief for this present series demanded analysis more than description, and allowed me to write not so much about Kuhn as about the sociological questions upon which he offers important insights. This is a book about the sociology of scientific knowledge which takes Kuhn's work as its point of departure. It provides no general intellectual biography of Kuhn, nor a comprehensive discussion of his significance as a philosopher, historian, or even sociologist. (Kuhn's sociological functionalism, for example, which actually finds expression in the titles of some of his papers, is not considered here.) It is what Kuhn has contributed to the social sciences that I discuss, how those contributions have been developed in recent years, and how they might usefully be further developed.

Since I look at Kuhn's work through the eyes of a sociologist, certain themes are highlighted and extended to their furthest limits; others are passed over. The result is something markedly divergent from the general drift of the numerous commentaries by philosophers and historians. This is not to say that it is necessarily better.

Conditioned as it is by narrow interests and objectives it can claim no special standing for itself. But where is the account that could claim such a standing? Even if Kuhn himself were to look back upon his earlier work and offer (as undoubtedly he would) a different framework within which to understand it, that would merely be yet another commentary, interesting and important certainly, but no touchstone of the significance of other accounts. All exegesis, even self-exegesis, is informed by specific aims and interests.

My aim here is to help sociologists to make profitable use of Kuhn's work. I do not attempt the task of regenerating his thinking. Nor do I take any interest in the precise extent of his own individual originality. None the less it is worth noting that Kuhn has made one of the few fundamental contributions to the sociology of knowledge. It fell to him to provide, at the time it was most needed in the 1960s, a clear indication of how our own forms of natural knowledge could be understood sociologically. This encouraged the empirical studies of scientific culture which were then beginning in the social sciences. And it inspired a revived awareness of the constitutively social character of knowledge generally — an awareness which had faded away in the post-war period. This is why a discussion of current views in the sociology of scientific knowledge can be developed from an examination of Kuhn's work, even though Kuhn himself is not a sociologist.

Having outlined the aim of the book, it only remains for me to offer some words of warning to the reader. First, I wish to ensure that the style of the text does not disguise how very little we know about learning, about credibility, and about our modes of inference. No writer dwells upon his own ignorance; there is no point. But as a result there are texts, whether in physiology, psychology, information theory, sociology or philosophy, which leave the false impression that they have penetrated to a deep understanding of how we come to know things. They even occasionally imply that the key to the matter lies in a single theory or a single field. I have no reason to assume that my own style could not create similar false impressions, so I seek to anticipate them here. In particular, I want to emphasise that a sociological approach can only be part of the larger project of gaining a proper *empirical* understanding of the characteristics of knowledge and cognition.

Second, although the various chapters of the book centre upon different topics, they cannot be taken as independent essays. The sociology of knowledge is among the least developed of all areas within the subject, and there are few routinely accepted ideas and assumptions which can be taken for granted as one writes. Accordingly, I introduce a number of generally useful ideas as I go along, attempting to explain them clearly on their first appearance and subsequently using them freely.

Finally, there is the statutory warning which must always accompany any thoroughgoing sociological treatment of science. When social scientists study scientific knowledge, the focus of attention is the knowledge associated with a specific social context. The question is why such knowledge is accepted as knowledge in the context. The answer must expose every sociologically interesting factor which has a bearing on this question. The assumption is that such factors are always involved in the network of causes which maintains the credibility of a body of knowledge. The plausibility of the assumption derives both from the merit of the work it inspires, and the glaringly obvious inadequacy of its converse, which denies that knowledge is a social phenomenon. The appropriate method of investigation is that accepted for the study of thought and action in general; in this case the thought is scientific thought and the action is research. This sociological orientation is very different from that of scientists themselves, who only explicitly consider how their knowledge relates to experience or to the performance of technical tasks. And it can lead to findings which contradict the self-images and forms of justification professed and accepted by scientists. There is no escaping the fact that sociological work could conceivably be employed in attempts to weaken some legitimations of science. But the sociology of knowledge is emphatically not, as its critics often mistakenly believe, itself a denigration of science; on the contrary, it is in many ways modelled upon scientific investigation, and any claims to credibility it comes to have must be closely related to those of science itself. The sociology of knowledge is a matter-of-fact, empirical field of study which happens to include, among its subject-matter, the knowledge and culture of science. It must examine that knowledge without any concern for the implications of its findings if it is to maintain its own integrity.

June 1980   Barry Barnes

Acknowledgements

I should like to express my gratitude to the many people who helped in the preparation of this book, and in particular to the staff and students at the Edinburgh Science Studies Unit for providing so suitable an environment in which to work and write. Michael Barfoot, Celia Bloor, David Bloor, David Edge, Anthony Giddens, John Law, Donald MacKenzie and Andrew Pickering all read earlier drafts of the manuscript, and helped me to identify and eliminate many weaknesses in substance and in presentation. Carole Tansley made light of the daunting task of producing a typescript from my initial handwritten material. And Moyra Forrest assembled an index incomparably superior to anything I myself should have been able to accomplish.

Figure 5.1 first appeared in *Centaurus*, vol. 3, 1953, p. 135; and I am grateful to the editors of that journal for allowing it to be reproduced here.

Author's Note

It is convenient to divide Kuhn's publications into three classes. First, there are concrete historical narratives, produced in the 1950s and the early 1960s, and addressed mainly to professional historians of science: particularly noteworthy here are *The Copernican Revolution* (1957), and a series of papers on the history of thermodynamics. Second, there are publications, beginning around 1960, which represent an attempt to understand science in general terms and to identify its distinctive features. This is the work through which Kuhn is most widely known, and in which most of his sociologically interesting ideas are to be found. It includes his book on *The Structure of Scientific Revolutions*, first published in 1962, but referred to here in the slightly longer second edition of 1970. And it embraces also a wide-ranging series of papers on historical, philosophical and sociological issues, many of which have recently been reprinted in *The Essential Tension* (1977). Wherever possible, when I expound or quote from Kuhn's papers, I give page numbers which refer to this readily available volume. Finally, there is work which reflects the detailed attention Kuhn has devoted in recent years to the history of quantum mechanics. *Black Body Theory* (1978) is the principal contribution to date of this kind. It is a fascinating and important work; but its central concern is to establish, through meticulous care and uncompromising attention to detail, a particular description and interpretation of a specific historical episode. Since *Black Body Theory* breaks new ground only as historical narrative, and deals with developments of daunting technical complexity, I do not discuss it here. Inevitably most of my citations relate to the wide-ranging and comparatively speculative material of what perhaps should be called Kuhn's 'second period'.

One matter of terminology also requires preliminary clarification. An important concept in Kuhn's work is that of the scientific *paradigm*. But in *The Structure of Scientific Revolutions*, where it is extensively employed, its meaning is not as clear and consistent as might be wished (cf. Masterman, 1970), and this has given rise to some significant misunderstandings. Kuhn (1970, Postscript) himself has recognised the problem and sought to eliminate it, but difficulties remain for anyone who would discuss the development of his work over a period of years. I have decided to use 'paradigm' to denote an accepted problem-solution in science, a particular concrete scientific achievement. This is the sense of 'paradigm' which, in his most recent work, Kuhn conveys by the term 'exemplar'. Purely as a matter of terminological decision, then, to which I try to adhere throughout, paradigms are exemplars.

B.B.

List of Figures

1

Traditions of Research

Before considering in detail the sociological implications of Kuhn's work, there is much to be said for a chapter which attempts a distant overview, a first reconnaissance of the intellectual landscape. It is particularly useful to be aware that Kuhn writes not as a sociologist but as a professional historian. Although he is known as the author of a 'theory of science', a vision of scientific change which is often compared with those of Popper or Lakatos, this can be misleading, and does him less than justice: his thinking is in the main much more concrete and empirical. Kuhn is indeed deeply involved with the general question of what science, scientific research as it is actually practised, is really like; but many of his methods and assumptions first appear as he seeks to unravel specific historical problems. Let us begin, then, with Kuhn's early papers on thermodynamics, where his historical methods can be seen in operation, put to work to answer particular questions. These methods are of sociological interest and continue to inform Kuhn's subsequent work.

All historians of science are agreed that one of the major contributions to thermodynamics, indeed the major initiating contribution, was made by the Frenchman Sadi Carnot in 1824. By considering a single cycle of an idealised heat engine, Carnot was able to derive a series of theoretical results closely paralleling those of modern, 'fully worked-out' thermodynamics; and this treatment of 'Carnot's cycle' proved to be an invaluable resource for those later generations of scientists who collectively established the modern theory. There is, however, one crucial difference between Carnot's results and those accepted today. Carnot held that 'calorique' or 'chaleur' (heat) was conserved in the operation of his engine; but the modern view is that the work done by an engine must be provided as energy from some source, and the source in this case is a loss of heat as the engine operates. The law of conservation of energy is assumed in modern thermodynamics, which suggests that the energy usefully extracted from the engine is balanced by a loss of heat energy within the engine: the engine converts heat into work. Hence the modern view is that heat is not conserved through the cycle of the engine: it is *entropy*, a distinct but related quantity, which is conserved. Carnot however, writing before the principle of the conservation of energy was clearly formulated and accepted, used a theory that took heat to be a material substance: to do this was to accept that heat was conserved, since the annihilation of matter was not then thought possible.

Apart from this point of difference, Carnot's and the modern view are in remarkably close analogy. If one takes Carnot's results and replaces 'heat' with 'entropy', one has to all intents and purposes the modern account. There is, in Carnot, the structure of modern thermodynamics; and yet in the last analysis Carnot's work seems to be erroneous.

This is sometimes thought a strange conclusion. It seems to imply that erroneously based reasoning played a crucial role in the establishment of one of the most successful areas of modern physical science. Accordingly, attempts to reinterpret Carnot's work are occasionally made. One suggestion is that when Carnot wrote 'calorique' he meant 'entropy', and that 'calorique' should be translated as 'entropy' and not as 'heat'. The implication is that Carnot was to some degree aware of the truth, that heat was energy rather than a material substance, and that he had an informal or implicit understanding of entropy as he wrote his essay of 1824.

Kuhn's first paper (1955) on the history of thermodynamics evaluates this possibility. He gives detailed attention to Carnot's text of 1824, and firmly rejects the suggestion that 'calorique' can be regarded as even loosely synonymous with 'entropy': 'calorique' is 'heat'. More interesting than the conclusion, however, is the method by which Kuhn arrives at it — the method, that is, which Kuhn employs in interpreting the historical material. His procedure implies a number of general assumptions which, in the absence of contraindications, guide his exegesis and understanding of Carnot's text.

First, it is assumed that the writer, in this case Carnot, is someone whose general mode of cognition is much the same as our own. His writings should be treated as internally coherent; they should make sense as a systematic presentation of ideas. The way a word is used in one instance should provide a good indication of how it is used in the next instance; a belief expressed in one context should be provisionally taken as a continuing conviction in subsequent contexts; a reading of a text which makes it self-consistent should be preferred to one which makes it self-contradictory — all this, of course, given the absence of specific contraindications. This principle is explicitly elaborated at a number of points in Kuhn's later work. For example, in the preface of his collected essays (1977, p. xii), he offers the maxim 'When reading the works of an important thinker, look first for the apparent absurdities in the text and ask yourself how a sensible person could have written them.'

Second, it is assumed that the usage of a writer is, in general, that of the culture wherein he is situated and with which he is interacting. The coherence of a body of writings is coherence between the meanings of the terms employed, meanings which are those current at the relevant time in the relevant context. It is important not to read back modern usage into an earlier context without being sure that the usage was indeed current in that context. Spurious contradictions can often be generated by lack of attention to this.

Finally, if one seeks to understand *why* specific beliefs are advocated or concepts employed in a text, all explanatory factors invoked must have been present in the actual historical context immediately beforehand. Causes must precede the effects they bring about; reasons must be present before the actions they inspire. This may well seem the most nearly self-evident of three unexceptionable assumptions; none the less it will soon be evident that there is real point in making it explicit.

Kuhn's analysis of Carnot's text proceeds smoothly on the basis of these assumptions. The contentious term 'calorique' is used in many contexts interchangeably with 'chaleur', which suggests that the two terms should be taken as synonymous. Nothing goes against this assumption; no internal contradictions or breakdowns of sense are produced by it. But the standard usage of 'chaleur' is translatable as 'heat': 'chaleur' meant 'heat', so 'calorique' also meant 'heat'. The identification is confirmed by Carnot's explicit statement that he uses the material theory of heat — a statement which becomes extremely puzzling if 'calorique' is rendered as 'entropy' and Carnot is assumed actually to have used the modern conception of heat as energy.

What, however, of the conclusions of modern thermodynamics? These are irrelevant to the understanding of Carnot's text, since they postdate it. It is true that the conception of heat as a form of energy, and not a material substance, was taking shape in early nineteenth-century Europe. It is true that Carnot himself discussed this theory, and even advocated it. But this occurred in writings set down *after* 1824. There is no evidence that Carnot proceeded on the basis of such a theory prior to 1824. In particular, there is no imaginative construction or step of inference in the text of 1824 which indicates the use of such a theory. Everything makes good sense on the basis of the theory which Carnot said he was using. Similarly, although *we* know of experiments and observations which seem to fit ill with the material theory of heat, there is no evidence that Carnot knew of any in 1824. Carnot's 'errors' could only have reacted back upon his thought if he had recognised them. But he did not. *Our views on the merits of Carnot's theory are of no historical interest.* It is Carnot's views and the context in which they arise which are relevant for historical understanding.

Kuhn's approach here is simply that now favoured by the vast majority of professional historians. Reacting against the Whig history once common, he takes the past as far as possible on its own terms, instead of setting it into a false relation with the present. Whig history treated the institutions of earlier generations as incompletely constructed versions of our own: their beliefs as partial representations of what is now fully understood; their innovations, whether in custom, social organisation, technique or natural knowledge, as movements towards the more 'advanced' forms found today. Historical change was preconceived as 'progress', and accounted for as a movement closer to the present. It was almost as though the present was a cause of historical change, pulling the past in conformity to it by some magnetic attraction, or perhaps pre-existing like some genetic code in the developing social organism, telling it the final perfected form into which it had to grow. Thus Whig history read the past backwards, finding its explanations in a later period than the events explained.

The modern professional approach which set this to rights is now long-established and fully accepted in practically every historical field. Its introduction into the practice of the history of science should perhaps be credited to Alexandre Koyré, a scholar to whom

Kuhn on many occasions acknowledges a major intellectual debt. But in the history of science Whig history persisted longer than in most fields, and indeed still continues. With science it can be peculiarly difficult to refrain from understanding the past in terms of the present. There is a continuing tendency to see the knowledge of modern science as the very pattern of reality itself, a pattern which has always existed, and hence which could have directly influenced the scientists of earlier generations. It is not always easy to remember that current science is our *interpretation* of reality, something which did not exist until we constructed it, and which cannot be projected back to operate as an underlying influence upon the perceptions of historical agents.

Fortunately, Kuhn's approach not only exemplifies good historical method, it is also exactly what is needed for sociological study. An anthropologist addresses the members of an alien culture just as Kuhn treats historical agents. He assumes that the alien discourse is coherent and meaningful; he seeks to understand it in its own terms, avoiding ethnocentric evaluations and misleading analogies with his own culture; he reads social and cultural change forwards from past to present. And just as the anthropologist seeks to understand an alien culture, so the sociologist seeks to understand the sub-culture of science — in its own terms, and from past to present. Sociology is a subject with a naturalistic, rather than a prescriptive or normative orientation; it simply tries to understand the convictions and the concepts of different cultures as empirical phenomena. External evaluation of the convictions and concepts is irrelevant to this naturalistic concern; all that matters is why they were actually sustained, at a particular time in a particular context. Like Kuhn, the sociologist cannot entertain the notion that our present-day conceptions of what is true or correct somehow have an influence on thought and judgement in other unconnected contexts. Kuhn's account of Carnot's work, which stands however that work is evaluated, as truth or error, as good inference or baseless speculation, is bound to appeal in its very form to those social scientists with an interest in scientific culture. It is a contribution to the understanding of that culture as a *phenomenon*.

Carnot's work puzzled people because it seemed so accomplished, so important, and yet so wrong. Kuhn did not share this puzzlement; yet, in a different way, he too was perplexed by the same material. It could be set into cultural context, but none the less it remained remarkably innovative, something which appeared to make a singularly far-reaching leap beyond existing precedent, a leap almost without parallel in the history of science and certainly unparalleled in thermodynamics: 'There is no single step in the history of thermodynamics so bold or so penetrating as the one made by Carnot. In particular, there is no step which carried its author so far from the main stream of contemporary scientific thought' (Kuhn, 1955, p. 94). Evidently Carnot did not fit quite snugly enough into the cultural context of his time.

A few years later Kuhn had resolved this problem and radically reformulated his view of Carnot in the process. Carnot's work is indeed startlingly original when set against the background culture of the physical science of his time. But this is not the appropriate background. Some years earlier a differentiation had occurred between physics and engineering, and their literatures had separated. Carnot's training was mainly in engineering, and it is against that background that his work is appropriately set. There are precedents for Carnot's work in the literature and the artefacts of power engineering, and Carnot was aware of them (Kuhn, 1960, 1961b). Carnot's work remains a brilliantly creative accomplishment, but by looking beyond the culture of science as narrowly conceived it is revealed as an intelligible development within a tradition of research.

Carnot drew a great deal from power engineering. His initial problem, that of deriving the greatest effect from a given expenditure of power in an engine, was a major theme in the engineering literature. Several of his concepts derived from the same source, and were not available in the scientific literature of the time in France; a notable example is the concept of work or mechanical effect. A number of generalisations and theorems about the behaviour of engines were probably also utilised. But Kuhn is concerned to stress, too, how the engineering tradition provided more than mere verbal formulations. In a manner typical of the whole of his work he looks for relevant concrete models and ways of structuring perception within the engineering tradition; and he finds them. There are idealised representations of engines in engineering texts which resemble representations in Carnot's work (Kuhn, 1960, p. 254); and there is an actual engine, known to Carnot, which in its very structure and operation offers a vivd image of one of the key processes with which Carnot had to deal (Kuhn, 1961a). Kuhn shows how Carnot synthesised a range of cultural resources, verbal and non-verbal, into a single powerful representation — the cycle of an ideal engine, the Carnot cycle. But Carnot's imagination did not create those resources from nothing; they derived from the engineering tradition.

Thus Carnot's work is finally made intelligible, as Kuhn always tries to make such work intelligible, by its relationship to a tradition of research — a sub-culture wherein research is carried out with a set of received procedures, representations and concepts, upon a set of received kinds of problems. This is now the standard orientation of historians to the work of individual scientists. Those who carry out scientific research are the recipients of a culture developed by previous generations. Research cannot proceed independently of it; its acceptance, however provisional, is a prior condition for doing science. The process of research in turn modifies and develops the received culture, and in this modified and developed form it is passed on to the next generation. The work of any individual scientist has to be understood against the particular cultural background surrounding him at his point of entry into the research tradition.

With this in mind it is interesting to consider Kuhn's two book-length historical studies, both of which focus upon episodes of revolutionary significance in the history of science. In the first, *The Copernican Revolution* (1957), a vast sweep of the scientific and intellectual culture of Europe is considered, in order to demonstrate the importance of the replacement of the earth-centred Ptolemaic cosmology by the sun-centred system of Copernicus. But Copernicus himself was no revolutionary figure. He has to be understood in the light of the tradition of research stemming from Ptolemy's *Almagest*. Copernicus's astronomical concerns were narrowly focused on technical problems; his methods, esoteric and mathematical, were those of the existing tradition; his innovation of giving motion to the earth was but a restricted departure from orthodoxy, made in order to resolve recognised difficulties in the Ptolemaic account. There is a sense, as Kuhn says, in which Copernicus was the first modern astronomer; but in considering his own individual contribution Kuhn's book none the less presents him as the last in the great Ptolemaic tradition (cf. Kuhn, 1957, pp. 181–4). Kuhn's more recent study of *Black Body Theory* (1978) is even more striking in its conclusions. This book centres on the work of Max Planck, remembered as the man who demonstrated the need for a discontinuous physics, and commemorated as the discoverer of the quantum of action, h, Planck's constant. Kuhn is not at all concerned to criticise or devalue Planck's achievement, but if he is right Planck's crucial work was a piece of *classical* physics, involving no recognition of the existence of discontinuity in nature. Only later, when others had made the need for it clear to him, did Planck reluctantly accept a discontinuous physics. His own most significant creative contributions are intelligible as continuing an existing tradition of research centred upon thermodynamics.

Kuhn's historical studies skilfully relate the accomplishments of individual scientists to the cultural contexts in which their research was carried out. And his historical methods are also good sociological methods. This, however, does not account for the particular attention sociologists have given to his work. When they finally turned to the detailed study of scientific research, there was a great range of historical material which was sensitive to the role of tradition and received culture. Kuhn's treatment of Carnot, even his treatment of Copernicus, was paralleled in most of its fundamentals by other historical studies.

Most historians at this time, however, addressed research traditions in ways which minimised the sociological value of the resulting work. First, they lacked real curiosity about tradition, culture and received knowledge; these things were referred to simply as means of making sense of the thoughts and actions of particular scientists. The centre of interest was the *individual*. The cultural context was invoked to make the behaviour of the individual scientist rational, rather as one might invoke his geographical context to make the behaviour of a navigator rational. Tradition was an accepted resource in explanation, but not something which itself demanded study. Second, because received concepts and beliefs were routinely used to explain the actions of individual scientists, there was a tendency to idealism in the history of science, just as there is always such a tendency in the history of ideas generally. Concepts, beliefs, principles were credited with inherent potency; they were thought of as autonomous entities with power or influence over men's minds. Cultural change was even, on occasion, conceptualised as the unfolding of the inherent implications of ideas. Such a one-sided conception, which ignored the power men possess to extend, adapt, modify or reject received ideas, was not acceptable in sociology.

In Kuhn's work, in contrast, tradition and received culture are foci for empirical curiosity. They are not catch-all explanatory concepts, but themselves demand investigation and understanding.

Hence, in reading Kuhn, one learns about the nature of tradition and of culture. And one is spared the worst excesses of idealist history; for although Kuhn does sometimes impute to ideas that which he should impute to people, he none the less recognises the crucial fact that research traditions are kept in existence by the activities of scientists themselves. Tradition is understood empirically, in terms of the causes and characteristics of human activity.

Good indications of his empirical approach are the extra-historical sources Kuhn cites as relevant to his general understanding of science. Perhaps the most notable is a monograph of Ludwik Fleck (1935), which has only recently become available in English translation (1979). This work anticipates many of Kuhn's ideas, which is possibly why it was largely passed over on its original appearance. The product of a medical scientist with a real care for the details of actual research, the stature of the book is now clearly evident. Not only is it probably the first ever empirical study in the sociology of scientific knowledge, it is a very good one at that, and one from which much can still be learned. A second important source is the developmental psychologist Jean Piaget. Kuhn often looks to his work to understand how scientific concepts are conveyed and acquired, unconcerned that children, not scientists, are typically the subjects of Piaget's research. Finally, Kuhn cites Ludwig Wittgenstein, whose later work ties the meanings of concepts to the manner of their actual employment within specific communities.

These sources reflect Kuhn's recognition that to understand the way a tradition develops one has to address the basis of human behaviour; moreover, what is involved is *social* behaviour, as much a sociological as a psychological problem. It is this insight, combined with his historical sensibility, which gives Kuhn's work its originality and significance. The continuation of a form of culture implies mechanisms of socialisation and knowledge transmission, procedures for displaying the range of accepted meanings and representations, methods of ratifying acceptable innovations and giving them the stamp of legitimacy. All of these must be kept operative by the members of the culture themselves, if its concepts and representations are to be kept in existence. When there is a continuing form of culture there must be sources of cognitive authority and control. Kuhn was initially almost alone among historians in giving serious attention to these features of science.

The result of this attention, which becomes increasingly general and theoretical in Kuhn's later work, is to display just how profound and pervasive is the significance of the sub-culture in science, and the communal activity of the organised groups of practitioners who sustain it. The culture is far more than the setting for scientific research; it is the research itself. It is not just problems, techniques and existing findings which are culturally specific; so, too, are the modes of perceiving and conceptualising reality, the forms of inference and analogy, and the standards and precedents for judgement and evaluation which are actually employed in the course of research. Science is not a set of universal standards, sustaining true descriptions and valid inferences in different specific cultural contexts; authority and control in science do not operate simply to guarantee an unimpeded interaction between 'reason' and experience. Scientific standards themselves are part of a specific form of culture; authority and control are essential to maintain a sense of the reasonableness of that specific form. Thus, if Kuhn is correct, science should be amenable to sociological study in fundamentally the same way as any other form of knowledge or culture.

Kuhn's general account of research and the growth of scientific knowledge was first published in 1962, as *The Structure of Scientific Revolutions* (henceforth referred to simply as the *Structure*). Several of the themes of this book will be considered in detail in later chapters. For the moment, however, it will suffice to note how it displays all the procedures of research — manipulative, cognitive and evaluative — as possessing a conventional, culturally specific aspect. Scientific investigation, so often described wholly in terms of the 'reason' and perception of the isolated individual and his experience, is presented as a complex interaction between a research community, with its received culture, and its environment. According to Kuhn, knowledge and competence in a mature science are transmitted in the course of a dogmatic and highly structured training, which inculcates an intense commitment to existing modes of perception, beliefs, paradigms or problem-solutions, and procedures. Such commitment is the prerequisite for *normal science*, the typical form of research in a developed field, which amounts to 'a strenuous and devoted attempt to force nature into the conceptual boxes supplied by professional education' (Kuhn, 1970, p. 5).

Normal science is the linchpin of the scientific enterprise; it is how knowledge is developed and accumulated nearly all the time. Yet it is in no way a radically innovative activity. On the contrary, it is very much a routine carrying on of a given form of scientific life, employing accepted procedures along the lines indicated by accepted standards, and largely assuming the correctness of existing knowledge. At no point is cognition intelligible as a manifestation of 'reason' or 'logic' alone; at no point does an addition to knowledge correspond purely and simply to a further aspect of reality itself. What it is possible to think and to know are to an extent pre-structured. Whatever attains general credibility does so through processes involving cognitive commitments, acquired through socialisation and maintained by the application of authority and forms of social control.

At times, periods of radical innovation do interrupt the flow of this normal research. Major procedural and conceptual reorientations do occur, and these Kuhn refers to as 'revolutions'. But these in no way amount to 'reason' breaking out of socially enforced bonds. Rather, they are transitions from one pattern of conventional, routinised practice to another. In the course of any spell of normal science anomalies accumulate, problems and difficulties which only arise because of the attempt to fit nature into the pattern defined by the existing orthodoxy. When the extent of anomaly gives rise to widespread unease and dissatisfaction with the existing framework of research, a period of crisis begins in which work becomes more speculative and loosely structured. Eventually practice rearranges itself around new procedures and new concepts which are thought to deal more adequately with the anomalies of the old scheme of things: a scientific revolution occurs, and creates the basis for a new sequence of normal science. It is never possible, however, once practice has been reconstructed, to produce any context-independent 'rational justification' for preferring the new to the old, any indefeasible proof of 'advance' or 'progress'. Concepts, theories and procedures are changed; problems are changed; criteria of judgement are changed, including criteria of what is to count as a problem and what as a solution to a problem; perception itself is modified, as is the basis of the scientific imagination. Nothing provides the essential stable anchorage for comparative evaluation. Revolutions separate incommensurable forms of scientific life.

The *Structure* stimulated a great deal of criticism and controversy. It is easy to forget today just how unusual and challenging the work was at the time of its initial publication. It was strongly at

[margin handwritten notes: "Revolution"; "No rational justification for preferring the new."]

variance, of course, with the myths and idealisations of science generally disseminated through society as a whole; it gave short shrift to the stereotype of the scientist as the open-minded, disinterested recorder of experience. But it was also a far cry from existing academic accounts of the general nature of scientific research, which at that time were produced almost entirely by philosophers of science. These accounts, as much as the general myths and images, lacked the social dimension which features so strongly in Kuhn's work. They sought to portray judgement throughout the history of science as sufficiently determined by 'logic' and experience; and in doing this they produced formalisations and idealisations of scientific theories scarcely recognisable as versions of their historical originals. The philosophers of science found a sociological form of argument alien and difficult to understand; and they found Kuhn's attempt to analyse scientific judgement by empirical historical study incompatible with their own *a priori* approach. Thus it is not at all surprising that they received Kuhn's book with scepticism.

One must, however, look beyond its unorthodoxy to understand the intensity of the interest and the frequent hostility which the work aroused. Natural science has a central position in modern society, and images of it are, among other things, emblematic symbols to which people are frequently highly sensitive. General orientations to the social organisation and the form of life of modern Western society are often expressed as evaluations of the scope and mode of validity of scientific knowledge. Consequently, the descriptive adequacy of an account of science may have less bearing upon its reception than whether the account is perceived to legitimate or to discredit scientific knowledge. And this was certainly the case when interest in Kuhn's book was at its height in the 1960s.

Even a superficial reading quickly reveals that the last thing which the *Structure* seeks to do is to initiate a critical attack upon natural science. None the less Kuhn's account was perceived by his audience as having unfortunate consequences. By introducing a social dimension, and relating the status of scientific knowledge to the contingent judgements of specific communities of people, Kuhn undermined a whole range of philosophical arguments designed to secure a privileged epistemological or ontological status for science. Like any thoroughgoing sociological account of scientific judgement, Kuhn's involved a form of relativism — something which always seems to inspire revulsion among philosophers. More specifically, as a description of how scientists actually operated, the account was generally agreed to be highly unflattering: long periods of dreary conformity interrupted by brief outbreaks of irrational deviance — this was one parody of Kuhn's view of the history of science. Hence Kuhn found himself lambasted by philosophers who knew, *a priori*, that science simply could not be as he described, and who saw worrying consequences in allowing that it could be. And he was praised by radicals who did not need to look to know that science was doctrinaire and coercive just as Kuhn seemed to be saying.

Nor did the style of the book do much to discourage this kind of appreciation. Admittedly, it was presented as an attempt to identify what was distinctively valuable and efficacious in the practice and organisation of research, and thus had the form of a typical apologia. None the less the *Structure* was, for its time, an extraordinarily matter-of-fact work. It wasted little effort upon justificatory polemic or upon setting out its author's personal values. And its language made no concessions to the scientistic prejudices of its likely audience. Analogies with theology, religious conversion and political revolution were used to convey aspects of the operation of science; but such was the squeamishness of many intellectuals that these associations produced alienation more often than illumination. Conversely, Kuhn omitted to make use of accepted ways of symbolising a positive commitment to science. In philosophical writings it is not uncommon to find assertions of the 'rationality' of science and scientists occurring in every other paragraph or so. In many cases the locution is more or less meaningless; but it serves as a symbol of the writer's positive evaluation of science, as a signal that justification is being engaged in, that legitimacy is being claimed for the thought or action described. This kind of indicator, however, was not to be found in the *Structure*, with the consequence that Kuhn, whose entire method is based upon the assumption that historical agents are reasonable men, was thought by philosophers to be accusing scientists of endemic irrationality (Lakatos and Musgrave, 1970).

Despite this, the *Structure* did elicit a number of positive responses, unconnected with any of its imagined iconoclastic implications. Among historians, sociologists and natural scientists themselves, there were several who were struck with the empirical plausibility of many of its claims; it was recognisable as a historically well-informed attempt to describe actual scientific activity in general terms. Thus, although the book indubitably gained its initial visibility for other reasons, once its themes were widely disseminated they came to serve as a resource and an inspiration for a number of different strands of empirical research.

The *Structure* was read with particular interest in the sociology of science, where its reception coincided with a rapid expansion and reorientation within the field. It was at this time that sociologists in the USA began to raise the magnification of the lens with which they studied science, and to examine the *specialty* as the characteristic social unit of research, the unit which engaged in the organised development of a specific body of knowledge and competence. In Britain and Europe, meanwhile, the sociology of science was becoming established for the first time, and here interest in scientific knowledge itself was strong, as well as in the nature and organisation of specialties. Kuhn's work was taken up in both these contexts.

Scientific specialties have been an important focus of research on both sides of the Atlantic over the last decade (cf. among very many examples Mullins, 1972; Mullins *et al.*, 1977; Edge and Mulkay, 1976; Lemaine *et al.*, 1976). Such work expresses a well-established interest in social organisation and social structure in a way well adapted to Kuhn's conception of how knowledge is socially ordered and communally extended. However, although Kuhn's work helps to define the objectives of this research, it does not provide it with its tools. Specialty studies may well have a bearing on how some of Kuhn's views are evaluated in the long term; but these studies employ methods imported from elsewhere in sociology and adapted as required. Kuhn himself has very little to say about the fine details of social organisation in science.

When, however, we turn to the other line of research, which has focused upon scientific knowledge itself, and the processes whereby it is generated, transmitted and sustained, things are very different. The methods used here are interpretative, and historical writings often figure prominently among the materials to be interpreted. Indeed, this kind of sociological work is now closely related to comparable activity in social and intellectual history. Not surprisingly, therefore, Kuhn's own ideas have been found particularly interesting in this context, and it is here that their sociological implications have been most frequently explored and developed (cf. Law, 1975; Bloor, 1976).

It could even be argued that work in the sociology of scientific knowledge has relied too heavily upon Kuhn, whose academic interests have after all not been identical with those of social scientists. Kuhn has not sought to develop sociological theory, or to understand knowledge and culture in the most general possible terms. On the contrary, his explicit aim has been to discover what is peculiarly distinctive and efficacious in scientific research, and he has tended to discourage the extension of his ideas to forms of culture other than science (cf. Kuhn, 1969).

Fortunately, this clash of objectives is less severe than might at first appear. The way to understand the peculiar efficacy of research was, as Kuhn saw it, to describe actual research as carefully and accurately as possible, as an empirical phenomenon. Hence his initial preconception, that science was somehow special, did not prejudice the status of his work as a descriptive, naturalistic account of science. Indeed, whether he recognises it or not, his description of science has called into question his preconception: at least in so far as sociologically interesting factors are concerned, it has revealed nothing fundamentally distinctive in the culture of science (Barnes, 1974). Again, although there are themes in Kuhn's account of science which belong there, and there alone, Kuhn's general sociological intuitions penetrate too deeply to be confined in their significance to one specific area. His treatment of the nature of convention, culture and tradition is so insightful, and far-reaching in its implications, that it should be essential reading for anyone with an interest in these subjects, whatever its specific focus. However, if I am to justify this claim, I must first examine Kuhn's views in proper detail, in the context to which they are intended to refer.

[handwritten margin note: nothing distinctive in the culture of science.]

2

Training

2.1 Pedagogy

Kuhn's account of scientific training is the thinnest and most weakly substantiated part of his general discussion of science. It is supported by no empirical research, and is not clearly related to his own special competences. This, however, only makes its importance the more remarkable. Previous views of scientific training had assumed that it involved genuine experimental validation and conclusive reasoning, that it enjoined openness to experience, that it encouraged a genuinely critical and sceptical attitude. Kuhn's account may have been thin empirically; but by denying all these earlier commonplaces, it revealed that they had no empirical basis at all. Kuhn's informal observations on how science is actually taught proved of great significance simply because they addressed a subject where genuine observations of any kind were rare.

According to Kuhn, if one looks at the extended training which precedes research in a developed scientific field, then its most evidently distinctive feature is the extent to which it relies upon textbooks: the accepted terminology of a field, its methods, its findings, its favoured modes of perception, are all conveyed through their use. And the credibility of all these components of scientific culture depends not upon the indications of experience lying behind the exposition of the text, but upon the authority of the teacher, and the institutional apparatus which supports it. Only this suffices to establish the standing of the particular way of ordering and manipulating the physical environment peculiar to the science in question. Scientific training is dogmatic and authoritarian, and it is hard to see how it could be otherwise. Since the neophyte initially lacks the competences and concepts of the scientific culture, he cannot evaluate it or criticise it in its own terms. He has to be regarded more or less as an apprentice. His native reasoning abilities, memory, dexterity, serve him as resources in acquiring expertise at this stage, not as means of interrogating nature. Even his perception must be appropriately channelled and structured:

> Looking at a contour map, the student sees lines on paper, the cartographer a picture of a terrain. Looking at a bubble-chamber photograph, the student sees confused and broken lines, the physicist a record of familiar subnuclear events. Only after a number of such transformations of vision does the student become an inhabitant of the scientist's world, seeing what the scientist sees and responding as the scientist does (Kuhn, 1970, p. 111).

Although it is invariably organised as a preparation for research, scientific training does not instruct students in the practice of research: it neither sets tasks with any really problematic dimension, nor shows how techniques can be combined and developed to overcome the difficulties which actual research may encounter. Instead, training concentrates upon the transmission of existing knowledge and procedure. It provides, it could be said, the cultural resources required in research, and simply presumes that the resources will be put to good use. Training does not generate or encourage traits such as creativity or logical rigour; rather, it equips scientists so that it is possible for them to be creative, or rigorous, or whatever else, in the context of a specific form of culture.

When we ask how *precisely* textbook-based training proceeds, and how knowledge and competence is passed on, we encounter for the first time what is perhaps the most important single concept in Kuhn's work, that of the scientific *paradigm*. As presented in a text-book, a paradigm is an existing scientific achievement, a specific concrete *problem-solution* which has gained universal acceptance throughout a scientific field as a valid procedure, and as a model of valid procedure for pedagogic use. Carnot's cycle has been adapted for use as a paradigm in this sense; so has Mendel's experimental work on inheritance in peas, Bohr's on the electronic orbits of the hydrogen atom, Crick's and Watson's on DNA. Further examples can be found by examining the standard texts of practically any

paradigms
& exercises

specialty in the physical and biological sciences.

Students work through paradigms with great care and in great detail; and then, either with pen and paper, or with laboratory facilities, they work through textbook exercises, all with similar structures and requiring similar procedures. In this way the structures of paradigms are thoroughly assimilated, and the procedures involved are mastered and become routine accomplishments. Kuhn makes the analogy with musical training. Although both musical performance and scientific research are in a sense creative activities, training in both involves the production of strong 'mental sets' or *Einstellungen* (Kuhn, 1963, p. 351). The exercises of the science textbook are akin to the finger exercises of the pianist, pedagogically preferable to the music of actual research. Just as the highly routinised manipulative skills acquired by finger exercises are exploited in the performance of a musical composition, so the highly routinised cognitive skills of the scientist are exploited in the puzzle-solving activity of research.

highly
routinized
cognitive
skills.

The culture of an established natural science is passed on in the form of paradigms. The central task of the teacher is to display them. The central task of the student is to assimilate them, and to acquire competence in their routine use. It is in this way, and not by purely verbal means, that the student gains a real understanding of what is known in his field. A proper understanding of the meaning of scientific concepts and the implications of scientific laws is only acquired by employing the concepts and laws in the course of carrying out paradigmatic procedures. Abstract verbal presentations of concepts, definitions, rules and laws are pedagogically unsatisfactory, and take second place in science to teaching through paradigmatic examples. Indeed, the most satisfactory way of describing scientific knowledge is simply as a repertoire of paradigms. To speak instead of an abstract pattern of concepts and beliefs, or statements, can be seriously misleading. (None the less I shall sometimes consider the verbal culture of science as an abstract pattern in just this way, since so much existing work proceeds upon this basis. On these occasions I shall refer to 'conceptual fabrics', and thereby make use of a metaphor which sometimes appears in Kuhn's own work (cf. Kuhn, 1964).)

proper under- standing requires use in carrying out paradigmatic procedures.

Scientific training always requires that a paradigm or paradigms be recognised as the sole legitimate representation of, and mode of dealing with, an aspect of the physical environment. It demands acceptance of the existing orthodoxy in a given field. Accordingly, it tends to avoid anything which might undermine or offer an alternative to that orthodoxy. The history of a field, wherein are found radically variant concepts, problems and methods of problem-solution, is either ignored, or is systematically rewritten as a kind of journey toward, and hence a legitimation of, present knowledge. Scientists, Kuhn says, are particularly vulnerable to the temptation to write history backwards and to depreciate historical facts, despite their very high regard for factual details of other kinds (cf. Kuhn, 1970, p. 138). Similarly, current but unorthodox perspectives and procedures are overlooked; and possible weaknesses, or even well-known and generally recognised difficulties in orthodox interpretations, fail to find their way into teaching texts. Textbook education demands concentration upon the components of one tradition to the exclusion of all others. It seeks to inculcate 'a deep commitment to a particular way of viewing the world and of practising science in it' (Kuhn, 1963, p. 349).

This view of scientific training and its consequences was sometimes found startling when it first appeared, and was read as critical commentary. It was offered, however, as an account of a well-ordered and effective regime, the existence of which helped to explain the 'success' of science (Kuhn, 1959). If science is conceived as a number of isolated individuals interrogating nature without preconceptions or biases, then Kuhn's account of training reads as an indictment. But if, as Kuhn correctly perceives, research is a collective enterprise of puzzle-solving, with the evaluation of findings depending upon conventionally based communal judgement, then authoritarian textbook-based training is an appropriate preparation for it. Standardisation of perception and cognition facilitates communication, organisation, interdependence and division of labour: the more dogmatic their training, the more scientists are bound together into a communal enterprise with all the familiar gains in efficiency which that entails. And just as dogmatic training effectively and beneficially binds the scientist to his fellows, so it effectively and beneficially relates him to nature. Nature is too complex for random, unsystematic, diffuse investigation. The consequence of the commitment encouraged by dogmatic training is that investigation is narrowed and focused, and is thus made more productive.

Moreover, commitment 'provides the individual scientist with an immensely sensitive detector of the trouble spots from which signifi-

cant innovations of fact and theory are almost inevitably educed'
(Kuhn, 1963, p. 349). A background of firm expectation makes
anomalies and exceptions stand out and take on significance; and it
is from anomalies and attempts to eliminate or assimilate them that
much successful scientific innovation stems. Thus Kuhn offers the
intriguing suggestion that innovation is encouraged by highly effective methods of socialisation, and that creativity may often be
regarded as a kind of conformity. This is a particularly valuable conjecture, since it is extremely tempting to assume that creativity is the
product of a flexible, open-minded, deviant or anti-authoritarian
individual, and thereby to associate the valued activities of innovation and creative synthesis with the valued state of the autonomous
agent.

Today, the general features of Kuhn's account tend to be
routinely accepted in sociology. How far scientific training is *particularly* authoritarian, and how far the specific 'success' of science is
thereby made more intelligible, remain open questions. But it is
recognised that Kuhn correctly describes training as a process of
socialisation. It transmits not the unique patterns inherent in physical nature but the patterns of conventions constitutive of a sub-
culture; it derives credibility not from proof or demonstration in the
sense of an inherently compelling sequence of inferences, but
mainly from authority and its manner of application. The consequence of training is not that impediments to proper perception and
inference are removed, but that specific competences in perception
and inference are acquired: socialisation provides the resources
appropriate to the practice of research.

There is, however, more to be retrieved from Kuhn's account
than an abstract formulation of what training involves: he displays
the specific ways in which it relies upon authority. A good example
here is his discussion of how science texts present theoretical predictions and experimental results (Kuhn, 1961a; cf. Kuhn, 1977, pp.
180ff).

Typically, predictions and results are set out in tabular form in
texts, in one-to-one correspondence with one another. There may
be two columns of numbers, with those on the left being predicted
values, and those on the right observed values, of some quanti-
tatively measurable phenomenon. Or there may be a graphical presentation, with a curve giving the predictions of a theory, and specific points the experimental results. The predicted values, the text-

book suggests, derive from theory. Certain general scientific laws or statements are taken, and combined with stated 'initial conditions' specific to a particular experimental situation. Logical and mathematical operations are then performed, to derive from the laws and conditions sets of predictions, P_1, P_2, P_3, etc. The actual results R_1, R_2, R_3, etc., are obtained by direct measurement in the course of the corresponding experiment. Since the measured values R_1, R_2, R_3 'agree' with P_1, R_2 and P_3 respectively, they confirm the theory in which the original scientific laws are included. Results deserve credibility because they are read off from reality, and thus presumably correspond to reality. Theory, in turn, deserves credibility because its predictions correspond with results. The text calls for commitment to a theory on these grounds.

Kuhn, however, is quick to point out that the actual credibility accorded to theories is not produced by the tables displayed in texts. The credibility of everything in texts derives from their status as authoritative sources. Predictions, results, and the relationship between the two, are all taken on trust by students because of the context in which they appear. Textbook tables do nothing to make the acceptance of theories more 'rationally justified'. Why, then, do such tables appear in texts? What, as Kuhn puts it, is their function (1977, p. 187; cf. 1970, ch. 11)?

His answer is this: rather than the agreement of the two sets of numbers confirming the theory, *it is the presentation of the two sets as being in agreement which gives an authoritative guide to what may be called 'agreement' in that context.* There is nothing in the inherent character of two different numbers to indicate that they are near enough the same, or significantly different. Nor (despite normal distributions and significance tests) are there means of dealing with all the approximations actually involved in theorising, and all the troubles habitually plaguing measurment, in such a way that a definition of agreement can be deduced. Agreement in science is always 'reasonable agreement', varying from context to context, and socially sustained. Textbook tables help to convey the accepted understanding of what is agreement, and hence help to lay down the conventional basis for the evaluation of research results. But they do it in an indirect way, which disguises their role and the character of the information they supply. (In allusion to the work of Emile Durkheim, it could be said that science texts encode messages about social relations in statements about nature. Whereupon it would have to be added that Kuhn displays admirable virtuosity in reading the code.)

2.2 Similarity relations

Many theories of knowledge are morality plays set in a Manichaean cosmos. The source of light is experience; its agent 'reason'. The source of darkness is culture; its agent authority. The remaining *dramatis personae* are garbed according to their origins. Truth, validity, rationality, objectivity are to be seen among the many white-apparelled children of the light; error and irrationality, custom, convention, dogma and many others are dressed in black. The moving principle of the drama is the unremitting conflict of the two opposed and irreconcilable forces.

There is nothing to be said in favour of this Manichaean mythology. Culture and experience interact at all times as knowledge grows; they operate symbiotically, as it were, not in conflict. None the less the myth is widespread and significant, and the habits of thought it favours must be taken into account. In particular, the term 'reason' is so widely understood as cognition and inference *without* a social component that there is little alternative but to give it this sense in what follows. The reader must simply understand that in asserting the insufficiency of 'reason' in science, the text will in no way imply that scientists are unreasonable men; rather, it will oppose an intolerably individualistic conception of cognition and inference. The argument will not be that something the opposite of what is reasonable or rational guides inference in science, but that the entire framework wherein the reasonable and the social stand in opposition must be discarded.

Let us now recall how Kuhn, in rejecting the textbook image of scientific knowledge, identifies it none the less as 'functional' (see section 2.1). It is functional not just because, as Kuhn says, it conveys information about convention or custom, but also because it conveys that information implicitly. The textbook image, by explicitly relating knowledge only to 'reason' and experience, maximises its authority and credibility in terms of the Manichaean myth: it relates knowledge only to the forces of light. Conversely, Kuhn's account, which explicitly invokes authority and convention, would be 'dysfunctional' as mythology.

Kuhn, however, is no Manichaean. At no point does his work suggest any conflict between culture and experience, authority and 'reason'. Kuhn takes it as a matter of course that the concepts and theories of science, far from providing conventional and hence inadequate accounts of the physical environment, are precisely conventional representations *of* that environment. We use our concepts and theories to group, order and pattern the objects and processes we encounter in nature according to their similarities and differences. There are any number of ways of carrying out this grouping and patterning. Those actually decided upon by a community, to the exclusion of others, are conventions of that community and have the backing of its authority: they constitute a socially sustained ordering of the environment, not a socially sustained distortion of it.

[handwritten margin note: Concepts & Patterns Socially chosen & sustained]

Let us expand these points using an illustration drawn from one of Kuhn's most extended and useful discussions of these matters (1977, pp. 307–19). The example is simplicity itself, yet by its very form it serves to set our thinking along the right lines. Kuhn considers a boy taking a walk with his father, in the course of which he will learn something of the different kinds of bird. We are to imagine that the child can already recognise birds, including some specific kinds of them; on the walk he will learn to recognise the hitherto unknown kinds, ducks, geese and swans. The child's father, who can be taken as a source of the accepted usage of his community, teaches that usage to the child by *ostension*. He points to particular birds and names them, say, as swans. When the child in his turn points to birds and identifies them as swans, the father confirms the identification, or rejects it: 'No, that's a goose.' Having seen a number of cited instances of 'swan', 'goose' and 'duck', and having himself practised their identification under the guidance of his parent, the child becomes himself competent in identifying the three different bird kinds. At this point instruction is completed; the child knows the three kinds of bird.

All the particular ducks, geese and swans encountered by the child and parent are unique entities. None are absolutely identical, but all bear some resemblance to every other. The birds exhibit an immense number of similarities and differences between themselves. None the less, at the end of the walk, they are ordered into three distinct clusters. The birds within any cluster differ from one another, just as birds of different clusters differ from one another. The birds of different clusters resemble each other, just as birds *swan example —*

within a cluster do. But the child has learned to highlight points of within-cluster resemblance and between-cluster difference. As a result of his striving to learn from his father, his cognition has fastened upon particular similarities and differences, and his perception may well have become modified to throw such resemblances and differences into relief: 'Part of the neural mechanism by which he processes visual stimuli has been reprogrammed' (Kuhn, 1977, pp. 309–10). It is this 'reprogramming' by exposure to particular instances of the terms 'swan', 'duck' and 'goose' that is the acquisition of knowledge of these kinds by the child, and the basis for his status as a competent language user in so far as those terms are concerned.

learned
similarity
relation

Each of the three clusters of particulars acquired by the child is what Kuhn calls a *learned similarity relation*. A system of such relations is an ordering set upon nature, not one insisted upon by it. The child might well have learned analogously constructed but none the less different orderings had he belonged to another community. Similarities and differences might have been exploited differently. (Anthropological fieldwork reveals the existence of such alternative natural kind classifications, and so does the history of science.) Hence what the child learns is the preferred arrangement of some community, rather than something insisted upon by nature itself. Nature does not mind how we make clusters from the vast array of similarities and differences we are able to discern in it: all that is required of such clusters is that they constitute a tolerable basis for further usage. The clusters are conventions; the similarity relations which concepts stand for are conventions.

Alternate
natural
kind classifi-
cations
(check).

None the less Kuhn insists that in learning such conventions knowledge of nature is increased. At the end of his walk the child can identify swans in his environment, and hence expect of particular identified swans whatever his community holds to be true or typical of them. By acquiring the communally sanctioned similarity relations, the child is able to apply the general knowledge of his community to particular situations in nature. The acquisition of culture gives the child a grip on experience.

Instead of talking of what the child has learned we can consider the process of learning itself. The learning process just described is a social process involving the application of authority. If the child finds that a bird resembles a swan, but has his identification 'swan' rejected, he does not oppose his own perception to that of his parent, and neither does he assume that his perception as such is at fault; rather, he assumes the irrelevance of the resemblance or analogy he has perceived, and seeks instead for differences which can justify the authoritative pronouncement of the parent. Without acceptance of an authority which transmits the conventional ordering, the child would be unable to learn even such simple descriptive terms as the kinds of birds. But the authority which is accepted serves to guide and form perception, and can only guide perception to the extent that nature is being adequately perceived. Authority cannot replace or override the perceptual apparatus of the child. It can serve only as a source of guidance as to how perception should be organised and conceptualised. During learning the social and the natural work together; culture and experience run in parallel; native cognitive capabilities and authoritative models in combination allow the acquisition of skill in concept application. The child cannot acquire his knowledge of bird kinds without parental assistance; but neither can he acquire it with his eyes shut.

Here, then, is an example which seems realistic and properly described, yet which goes against the central features of Manichaean mythology. Moreover, the form of the example is that of learning by ostension generally; ostensive learning confounds the Manichaen myth. Why then is this not more generally recognised and stressed? There are many causes, but none of them would have any efficacy were it not possible for us to conceive of learning in another way — as purely a process involving words. We tend to forget about ostensive learning in our obsession with learning as the acquisition of rules and definitions. There is a verbal bias in the sociological imagination. To learn a concept is too readily equated with being told what it means; ostension, if it is considered at all, is treated as an inferior and eliminable alternative. We shall find, however, that if one mode of learning is to be set below the other, then learning by rule and not learning by ostension must be allocated this secondary status.

It might be suggested that the parent in the example above should have transmitted the meaning of 'swan' verbally instead of by ostension: that a definition along the lines of 'a swan is a large, white-plumaged, orange-billed bird' would, if suitably elaborate and precise, convey the meaning without any parental act of concept application having to be taken on authority, and without the intrusion of social or conventional elements. Similarly, it might be

[margin annotation: authority guides organization of perception]

suggested that all other terms in the language should be learned by rule and not by ostension. Such a conception of language learning fits very neatly with Manichaean mythology. With every term there come verbal rules which tell the recipient of the term how it is to be applied. The individual recipient, if he is moved by 'reason', uses the term in the way the rules command. On the other hand, if the individual breaks the rules, then something must be overriding his rational tendencies, social pressures perhaps, or cultural biases.

Kuhn's own response to this account of learning is simply to argue that it does not always apply. Processes of ostension are frequently involved in knowledge acquisition, and have particular significance in natural science. They are, moreover, a form of knowledge acquisition with practical advantages over learning by rule and definition (cf. Kuhn, 1977, pp. 307–19); and thus they cannot, without loss, be replaced by processes solely involving rules and definitions. Perceptions of similarity learned by ostension will typically be part of the structure of knowledge, and will introduce a conventional character into that structure.

However, this way of justifying the importance of learned similarity relationships is too modest and limited, and can create a false impression. Learning by ostension and learning by rules and definitions are not competing strategies between which a choice is always possible. Learning by ostension is not something requiring serious consideration merely because natural scientists frequently give profitable employment to this option. Knowledge is not social here and there only — where recourse to ostension introduces learned similarity relations. Kuhn is too conciliatory to an inadequate image of knowledge, and thus fails to push home the full impact of his concrete example.

Kuhn's example showed terms being learned directly, by a social process of interaction with a physical environment, and with little or no involvement of existing language. Imagine, however, that verbal rules, or definitions like the one above, had been utilised in the learning process. Certainly, such statements could have assisted learning. But they could not have done so unless the terms they contained, 'white', 'plumaged', etc., had been informative. The child would have had to know already what these new terms meant, or how the terms were properly used. But there are no terms for which meaning or use is self-evident; nor does meaning accompany a concept as a mysterious halo. Hence any use of rules and definitions in conveying meanings either relies upon earlier ostensive acts of learning, or generates the further problem of the meanings of the terms in the rules. These problems may in turn be resolved by appeal to more rules and definitions, but this strategy alone would lead to an infinite regress. 'Swan' may be acquired by reference to 'white'; 'white' by reference to 'colour'; 'colour' by reference to . . . ; but such a sequence has to end with an ostensively learned similarity relation, a finite cluster of accepted instances of some term.

We can now see how false is the contrast between learning by ostension and learning by use of definition and rule. The real contrast here is between learning which relies *directly* upon ostension, and that which relies upon it *indirectly*. Nothing can be learned *ab initio* purely by verbal means. The child may learn 'swan' directly, or (for example) via 'all swans are white', which connects with previous processes of ostension involving 'white'. It follows that *all* systems of empirical knowledge must rely upon learned similarity relations transmitted by ostension or practical demonstration, and that what any given term in such a system refers to can never be characterised without reference to learned similarity relations, i.e. to finite clusters of accepted instances of terms. Knowledge is conventional *through and through*. If we understand the concept of the learned similarity relation, we thereby begin to understand in a profound and highly general way how nature and culture are intertwined in the generation of knowledge. Kuhn's discussion of this concept has a value and significance greater even than he himself has so far indicated. His work does not merely show that knowledge involves conventions and is taught as convention: it also enables us to see that knowledge must always have a conventional character, and it helps us to understand what it is for knowledge to have such a character.

2.3 Finitism

Kuhn's example has led to interesting conclusions, but its value is far from exhausted. We can employ it to consider what determines the proper usage of an empirical term. Given the argument immediately above, it is sufficient to consider similarity relationships, and to ignore the role of verbal generalisations or definitions. Ultimately, any constraints upon usage must derive from similarity

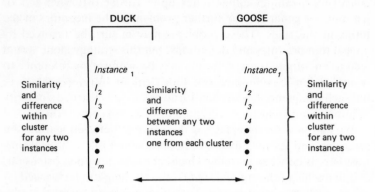

FIGURE 2.1   *Two similarity relations*

relations, given by ostension or by any analogous process which can link a term directly to experience. Accordingly, let us consider the state of affairs in Kuhn's example when full linguistic competence with respect to the similarity relations 'duck' and 'goose' has been attained (see Figure 2.1).

It is the pattern of the resemblances between the instances in the two relationships which it is crucial to grasp. The instances in each cluster differ from one another, even though, being ducks or geese, they are in that sense the same. Instances in different clusters resemble one another, even though, being differently labelled, they are in that sense different. Any putative new instance will at once differ from, yet be similar to, the instances in both clusters. This is the pattern which invariably emerges from ostension and analogous modes of learning. There are no clearly identical, indistinguishable particulars to cluster together. For all the complexity and richness of language, experience is immeasurably more complex, and richer in information. Physical objects and events are never self-evidently identical or possessed of identical essences.

It follows that past experience and the past usage of a concept can never suffice to determine future usage. When an individual confronts a putative new instance of a term, he confronts an array of similarities and differences, between the new and the past instances, and among the past instances. Formally, his assertion that an instance falls under a term is only his contingent judgement to the effect that similarity outweighs difference. Past usage offers precedents for his usage, but is not sufficient to fix it because there is no natural or universal scale for the weighing of similarity against difference.

Analogously, accepted usage within a specific community can be no more than agreement in the practice of the community. If an individual subordinates his inclinations to the routinely accepted mode of use of a term, it is to the practice of his fellow men that he defers, not to any set of rules or instructions for use which, as it were, come with the term. Proper usage is simply that usage communally judged to be proper, and is no more predetermined than idiosyncratic individual usage. Concepts cannot themselves convey to us how they are properly to be used. We ourselves must always agree or seek to agree that the application of a term to an instance is justified, that similarity should outweigh difference in that case.

This talk of judgement and agreement is no mere rhetorical exaggeration. A combination of our nature as organisms and our social experience often gives us like habits of concept application, and ensures agreement between us in particular situations providing only that we unthinkingly use language in the 'routine' way, the way that seems 'natural'. But to follow habit in this way is in no sense necessary; and it is certainly not something which concepts themselves enforce upon us. Moreover, there are always situations where no routines appear to be applicable, where nothing seems the 'natural' concept, where unthinking, automatic response is not possible. In such situations standard usage must be actively developed and extended in the course of social interaction; further linguistic routines must be laid down. Is deuterium oxide water? Is nine-carat gold to be classed as gold? What of eight-carat, or seven-carat? Is totemism a religious practice? Any term is liable to be involved in negotiable issues of this kind. Where the negotiations produce agreement, what results is a convention, a new routine. And although the new routine may assist a community in its dealings with nature, nature itself sets no constraints on the form of the routine which is produced. Any way of developing the accepted usage of a concept could equally well be agreed upon, since any application of a concept to an instance can be made out as correct and justified by the invocation of an appropriate weighting of similarity against difference. However unattractive and *ad hoc* such a justification may appear, it need never encounter any formal problems of consistency (cf. the extreme example in Hesse, 1974, ch. 3).

If present usage involves judgement and the achievement of agreement, then so too did past usage. Hence past usage is *revisable*: we may hold that 'wrong' judgements were made in the past. An existing standard instance of 'duck' may be agreed to be a moorhen after all; the pattern of similarity and difference which justified the one attribution may be said to justify the other even better. Note, too, the options available in glossing such a revision of usage. We could say that we have changed the meaning of our concept 'duck'. Or we could say that the meaning remains unchanged, and that incorrect usage has been detected and set to rights. Meaning changes, or stays the same, as the community wishes to have it.

In summary, then, concept application is a matter of judgement at the individual level, of agreement at the level of the community; it is open-ended and revisable. Nothing in the nature of things, or the nature of language, or the nature of past usage, determines how we employ, or correctly employ, our terms (cf. Barnes, 1980).

But if nothing external determines what concepts are to refer to, then nothing external determines the truth or falsity of verbal statements. If concept application is a matter of contingent judgement, then so too must be the processes whereby generalisations are confirmed or refuted. If what a duck is depends upon future judgements, then the truth or falsity of 'all ducks have webbed feet' as an empirical claim also depends upon future judgements. This leads directly to a radical view of the conventional character of knowledge. It is not that knowledge is a system of conventions which determines how we think and act. On the contrary it is our decisions and judgements which determine what counts as conventional, and thus which sustain and develop a conventional framework. To say that knowledge is conventional does not mean that evaluations, for example of 'truth', are 'system-dependent', or 'theory-dependent', or only relevant 'within a framework'; it means that such evaluations depend on *us*.

This conception of knowledge is sometimes called *finitism* (cf. Hesse, 1974, chs 8 and 12). Its core assertion is that proper usage is developed step by step, in processes involving successions of on-the-spot judgements. Every instance of use, or of proper use, of a concept must in the last analysis be accounted for separately, by reference to specific, local, contingent determinants. Finitism denies that inherent properties or meanings attach to concepts and determine their future correct applications; and consequently it denies

that truth and falsity are inherent properties of statements. 'True'
and 'false' are terms which are interesting only as they are used by a
community itself, as it develops and maintains its own accepted
patterns of concept application.

The significance and implications of finitism are perhaps best *extensional*
considered in relation to its opposite, which in Figure 2.2 is labelled *semantics*
'extensional semantics'. On this view, an empirical concept is either
true or false of all things in the spatio-temporal universe. It divides
that universe cleanly into two parts, being true of the constituents of
one part and false of the other. The set of things of which it is true is
sometimes called the 'extension' of the term (the 'reference' of a
term is a closely related expression, and is sometimes used interchangeably with 'extension'). Thus to talk of the extensions of terms
is to imply that future proper usage is determined in advance, that
everything already lies either within or without the extension of a
term. The individual finds out, by observation and 'reason', which
of these two alternatives appertains in any particular case, and
hence what constitutes proper usage. By behaving as a rational
automaton, without discretion, he conforms to correct usage.
Correct usage accordingly is of no sociological interest, being
merely a manifestation of 'rationality'.

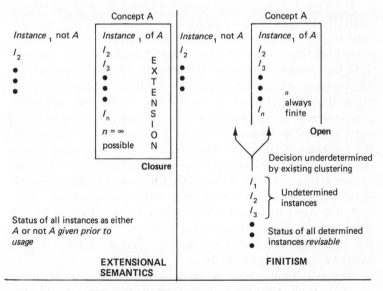

FIGURE 2.2 *Two semantic theories*

In contrast, finitism does not presume that any such entity as an extension is associated with a concept, and hence denies that correct usage can be discovered or inferred. Instead it opens all instances of concept application, and all acts of acceptance or rejection of applications of concepts, to sociological study as contingent judgements.

Consider, for example, some of the recent debates concerning the proper use of human gender terms. Governing bodies in athletics have shown interest in distinguishing 'genuine' females from pretenders to the title, and have turned to cyto-geneticists and other scientific specialists for assistance (which has been less forthcoming than they expected). From one point of view the problem here is to *discover* who is included within the extension of 'female' and who is not. The debate is a technical one concerning *XX* karyotypes, hormone levels, anatomy, and how reliable these things are as indicators of whether someone is or is not 'really' female. 'Female' has an extension fixed in advance, and the problem is to find out who falls within it. On a finitist view, however, efforts are being made here to *develop the usage* of 'female' and to *invent* new routine applications of the term for a specific context. It is pointless, save as a strategy in the context of discussion itself, to assume that athletes already fall into, or outside, some previously given extension of 'female'.

There is a debate among philosophers of science with a closely related structure, but concerning theories rather than single concepts. Important arguments about the status of scientific theories hinge upon what things or events they properly apply to. It is sometimes said, for example, that classical mechanics applies everywhere, to all bodies, in all contexts, under all conditions. This implies that classical mechanics is a false theory, since it generates erroneous predictions for the motions of bodies travelling close to the speed of light: classical mechanics applies to these bodies, ought to predict their motions, but does not. There is, however, a counter-argument to this, which questions whether classical mechanics actually 'ought' to predict these problematic motions. Classical mechanics, it is said, developed in relation to slow-moving bodies (relativistically speaking); it applies only to such bodies, and it does satisfactorily predict their motions. Hence classical mechanics is a true theory. That it fails for fast-moving bodies merely indicates that it is a theory of *restricted scope*, not that it is false.

Here is a dispute about the truth or falsity of a scientific theory which turns upon the issue of what the theory applies to. The two sides point to different determinate domains of application for the theory. But these domains are just like the extensions of simple empirical terms, and just as non-existent. The applications of a theory do not exist prior to acts which are the applications.

It might be said that scientists *intended* that classical mechanics should apply everywhere, and that they implicitly defined the scope of their theory by their intentions. But this would be a misconception. Only by examining a sequence of particular applications of classical mechanics, by scientists believing it to 'apply everywhere', would one get any idea of what it was, as far as they were concerned, for the theory to 'apply everywhere'. How, for example, did these scientists treat magnets, or light? To 'apply everywhere' is as negotiable and revisable a notion as any other; hence to use the notion to describe the intentions of scientists is of no help in fixing a domain of application for classical mechanics.

In any case, individual scientists vary in their intentions, and the same individual may change his intentions at any time as and when he employs a theory. Many scientists hold that their theories 'apply everywhere'. Others are instrumentalists, and take the scope of their theories as a matter for unending empirical investigation. Conflicting attitudes can be taken by different individuals or groups to the same theory. And at any time a change of viewpoint may occur, from one extreme to the other, without inconvenience at the level of research practice. However, then, can one hope to derive a determinate set of applications from intentions, when intentions are at best variable, heterogeneous and revisable? (Those who have experienced the sheer empirical difficulty of studying intentions often take a far more negative view even than this, and regard intentions as inaccessible, or even non-existent.)

Classical mechanics is not a false theory which applies everywhere; and neither is it a true theory of restricted scope. Like all theories, it has no predetermined set of applications, no given scope or domain; and hence, from the outside, it is pointless to label it 'true' or 'false'. That one or other label must apply is a gratuitous assumption. It is difficult to exaggerate the importance of this gratuitous assumption, and the far-reaching consequences of rejecting it in favour of a finitist approach.

If one studies concept application empirically, one tends quickly to notice its open-ended character, and the difficulties involved in applying such notions as that of extension. It is not surprising, therefore, that finitism has developed in a number of different guises in the social sciences, and that the question in that context is which precise form of finitism is the most satisfactory. Conversely, philosophers, whose objectives are usually evaluative rather than empirical, have tended to avoid finitist positions, which create difficulties for many of their central evaluative activities. One cannot unproblematically separate truth and error if one accepts finitism. Nor can one demarcate rational and irrational individuals according to how they apply concepts. And, perhaps the greatest disaster of all, finitism implies that there is no perfect solution to the problem of *translation*, and thus sets severe restrictions upon the comparative evaluation of different forms of knowledge and culture.

All attempts to achieve a perfect translation of a concept seek to match the inherent properties of the concept with the inherent properties of concepts in the second language. Correspondences are sought between the extensions and intensions of two concepts, or their references and senses, or their denotations and connotations. But finitism calls the existence of such properties into question. Not only does it thereby undermine standard methods of matching the concepts of two languages, it also indicates difficulties in equating the meaning of a single term at one point of use with its meaning at the next, when the similarity relation will have changed. From a finitist perspective, the between-system translation problems to be discussed later in relation to incommensurable scientific paradigms constitute but a special case of a much more far-reaching problem. All the problems of translation encountered where two cultures, and two languages, are involved have analogues in the case of the temporal development of a single system of culture. Small wonder, then, that philosophers avoid finitism.

None the less some invaluable insights into what I have called finitism are to be found in philosophical writings, and in particular in the work of Ludwig Wittgenstein (1953, 1964). It is unusual to find finitist approaches, whether in sociology, anthropology, ethnomethodology or philosophy, which do not draw upon him (cf. Garfinkel, 1967; Bloor, 1973; Douglas, 1973; Hesse, 1974; Phillips, 1977). Similarly, in Kuhn's work those discussions which link most closely to a finitist position refer back to Wittgenstein (cf. Kuhn, 1970, ch. 5), and Kuhn's sensitivity to the problems of concept application pointed out by Wittgenstein give his work an enhanced sociological interest. It is not clear whether Kuhn himself should be

characterised as a finitist (cf. Stegmüller, 1976, for relevant interpretations of Kuhn; and Kuhn, 1975, for comments upon Stegmüller); but neither is it of any importance. What is important is that
Kuhn's work, and specifically his discussion of learned similarity
relations, lends support to a finitist position, and helps us to see how
knowledge can be understood in this sociologically interesting way.

2.4 Finitism in physical theory

A finitist account of knowledge is justified wherever the acquisition
of knowledge relies upon learning processes of an ostensive kind. It
was argued in section 2.2 above that these processes are essential
throughout the realm of empirical knowledge, since without them
terms remain unconnected with phenomena and hence can convey
no information. None the less the implication that finitism gives a
correct description of, say, theoretical physics, as much as natural
history, remains hard to accept. These two domains of empirical
knowledge are generally perceived as fundamentally different: the
taxonomies of natural history are often agreed to be conventional
and revisable, as required by a finitist account, but the concepts of
physics are generally considered to differ from those of natural history on precisely this point. It would be wrong to abandon this
accepted contrast, and to recognise the fundamental sociological
equivalence of knowledge in physics and in natural history purely on
the basis of abstract argument. Part of the value of Kuhn's work is
that it helps us to compare the two forms of knowledge in a more
concrete way. Kuhn is one of the few writers who attempts to
describe the actual processes whereby physical concepts are connected directly to natural phenomena. And his description of these
processes runs in close analogy with the previous discussion of
natural-kind terms.

Just as the use of terms like 'duck' and 'goose' must be learned via
particular instances, so, says Kuhn, the use of the concepts of physics must be learned via accepted problem-solutions or paradigms.
This is precisely why problem-solving on the basis of given paradigms or exemplars is such a prominent feature of scientific training:

> Acquiring an arsenal of exemplars, just as much as learning sym-
> bolic generalisations, is integral to the process by which a student

gains access to the cognitive achievements of his disciplinary group. Without exemplars he would never learn much of what the group knows about such fundamental concepts as force and field, element and compound, or nucleus and cell (Kuhn, 1977, p. 307).

Just as competence with regard to 'duck' involves familiarity with a finite cluster of instances of 'duck', so competence with, say, 'compound', or 'force', or 'speed', involves familiarity with a finite cluster of problem-solutions (paradigms, exemplars) wherein the use (and thus the 'meaning') of the terms is directly displayed. And just as consideration of the finite cluster that is the similarity relation 'duck' leads to a finitist account of its use, so can consideration of the finite cluster of exemplars associated with physical concepts establish how finitism properly describes the use of concepts in physics.

The nature of a physical concept as a cluster of exemplars is particularly well illustrated with regard to 'speed', in one of Kuhn's most insightful papers (1964). Kuhn starts with Aristotle's *Physics*. Here, he tells us, motion is conceived of as a change from one state to another, i.e. as a total, completed movement. And 'speed' is usually discussed in relation to this particular conception of motion: 'The quicker of two things traverses a greater magnitude in an equal time, an equal magnitude in less time, and a greater magnitude in less time.' This Aristotelian concept of speed is very close to what today we should call 'average speed'. In their famous race, it would be appropriate in Aristotelian usage to say that the speed of the tortoise was greater than that of the hare; similarly, we ourselves would say that the average speed of the tortoise was the greater.

There are, however, other passages in the *Physics* where Aristotle speaks of the speed of a thing at an instant, or at least without any reference to the end-points of a complete motion; for example, he talks of things very rapidly gaining or losing speed. In these passages 'speed' appears to be something very like what we would call 'instantaneous velocity'. To us, such a concept is distinct from that of 'average speed'; there were, for example, many points in their race where the speed of the hare — in the sense of instantaneous velocity — was greater than that of the tortoise; indeed, the hare's instantaneous velocity was the greater for practically the whole of the period when it was actually moving. But, although we make much of this distinction, Aristotle fails to make it at all; examples of the 'average-speed' type and of the 'instantaneous-velocity' type fall together under his term for speed. Exemplars of the Aristotelian term differ from each other, just as instances of our natural history terms do. And Aristotle does not explicitly verbalise the differences, just as some differences always remain unverbalised between the instances of our modern natural kinds.

Those particular differences which we now routinely perceive between Aristotle's instances, by virtue of our possession of the concepts of 'average speed' and 'instantaneous velocity', were labelled and differentiated in a process of cultural change involving the mechanical theorists of the medieval period and culminating in the work of Galileo. Galileo demonstrated how important such a diffentiation of concepts was by imagining circumstances where difficulties arose if it were not made. Galileo imagined thought-experiments which encouraged conceptual differentiation in the mechanics of his time.

The race of the hare and the tortoise could be used as a thought-experiment in relation to Aristotelian physics. It would be perfectly possible for a culture to adhere to Aristotle's notions and yet to understand, or even to know as a matter of lore, the story of the race. Thus it could occur to someone to use the story to raise problems: look at the hare, is it not the faster of the two? — and yet it is the tortoise that is the faster, for it gets there first! There is good Aristotelian precedent for saying that the hare is both faster and yet less fast than the tortoise. This is inconsistent. More to the point, it is confusing and inimical to effective communication. Aristotelians, talking of the race together, could encounter difficulties in exchanging ideas and information; and they might, in the light of this, decide to change their usage. The thought-experiment might encourage cultural change.

This is not precisely how Galileo himself dealt with the problem of speed, but his own thought-experiment was not very greatly different, and as far as the formal features of interest here are concerned it was not different at all. Just as in the above, Galileo used different standard exemplars of the existing conception of speed to generate conflicting conclusions in a specific case. The result was to persuade people of the utility of regrouping the standard examples into two clusters.

Thus 'speed' in Aristotelian physics is a similarity relation, a cluster of instances between which there are differences as well as similarities. All that remains is to show why this example can stand as a typical instance of a concept of physics, and a good case for the general relevance of finitism will have been made. At first sight this final task might seem difficult. It might appear that Aristotle was confused in his thinking about motion, and that his concept of speed, far from being scientific, was exposed and rejected by the more analytical thinking which came with the rise of science. Scientific criticism, it might be said, revealed contradictions in Aristotle's concept.

This diagnosis, however, is convincingly rebutted by Kuhn. There was no contradiction in the concept. People were persuaded to discard it, or to differentiate it, *by reference to the real world*. If physical reality had been different, the Aristotelian concept could have continued in use without difficulty. For example, in a world where objects were always observed to pass from the beginning to the end of a motion at a uniform speed, the Aristotelian concept would have functioned satisfactorily; the hare—tortoise example would have been an impossibility. Thus, if we are willing to talk informally of the inherent properties of concepts, we should say not that Aristotle's concept was contradictory, but that it was *false* (cf. Kuhn, 1977, p. 258). Better still, we should simply say that actual situations were pointed to wherein usage of the concept generated *practical* difficulties and ambiguities.

The important point here is that *until* such situations are pointed to usage may be confident, straightforward and unproblematic. Kuhn draws a parallel with some experiments of Piaget upon the learning of children. At a certain point in their development children appear to relate their concept of speed to two kinds of experience: one experience is of an object getting to a goal before another — that object is the faster of the two; the other experience is a direct apprehension of rapid movement through, for example, a blurred spatial image. What eventually differentiates these kinds of experience is exposure to situations where rapidly moving objects reach a goal *after* less rapidly moving ones. To attain a fully differentiated 'adult' notion of speed, the children must be exposed to this kind of situation, so that they can recognise the difficulties it creates for their existing concept. Only then do the children become confused, and motivated to the modification of their existing usage.

How far, then, are our physical concepts like those of Aristotle, or those of Piaget's children, given that our own confidence in their use, and lack of any awareness of confusion and contradiction in them, is beside the point? There is every reason to think that they are much the same — that they embrace instances differing in detail from one another, and that future circumstances could arise which would encourage us to differentiate the instances into smaller clusters to avoid practical problems. Let us review the evidence for this. First, there are the indications from developmental psychology that as children we acquire physical concepts via familiarity with clusters of concrete instances, just as we acquire concepts like 'duck' and 'goose'. Then we have Kuhn's own informal description of the role of paradigms and concrete problem-solutions in scientific training: if our understanding of physical concepts does not reside in specific known instances of use, at least it seems to be acquired through such instances. We also know that many of the physical concepts we routinely and securely use can be further differentiated, and sometimes must be for clear communication. 'Velocity', for example, can often be used as it stands, but in many contexts it is crucial to distinguish absolute from relative velocity. Hence we know that the routine use of 'incompletely differentiated' concepts is a straightforward and commonplace matter in the context of modern scientific culture. Finally, we know that many concepts once considered to be beyond further differentiation or revision have in fact proved to have the character of Aristotle's speed concept. The history of science shows this clearly. Kuhn himself cites the way thought-experiments by Bohr, Einstein and Heisenberg revealed the composite and *ex post facto* confused character of notions of time, simultaneity, space and position. Given this, it seems inductively sensible to assume that our physical concepts are just like those of our ancestors. Even if we intuitively take some of our present concepts as fundamental, it is surely unwise to assume that in new situations they will not be treated as finite clusters of instances which can profitably be regrouped or differentiated. Thus there is very substantial evidence as well as powerful abstract argument in favour of a finitist account of concept application in physics, and, by extension, through the realm of empirical knowledge generally.

Finitism implies a thoroughgoing sociological treatment of knowledge and cognition. Conversely, any attempt to refute such a sociological treatment tends to a denial of finitism; and to the imputation of power and agency to concepts themselves, instead of to those who apply them. Talk of extensions or essences is the usual result. Kuhn's work stands as a major contribution to the social sciences if only because of its utility in the comparison of these alternatives.

3

Research

3.1 Discovery

The knowledge acquired from a scientific training is indeed knowledge of nature; yet at the same time it is a system of conventions. This is true of verbal as much as of procedural knowledge: scientific concepts constitute systems of conventions. Moreover, these conventions do not determine the cognition of those who acquire them, or even of those 'reasonable' individuals who acquire them. Our sense of what is conventional derives from our communal cognitive activity, and not vice versa. Conventions are the products of cognitive processes involving contingent judgements and agreements, and are continued and developed through further cognitive processes of the same kind. It follows that to understand scientific research we must maintain at every point a deep curiosity about ourselves, as well as about the natural environment.

In our society most accounts of research and the growth of knowledge have focused upon nature to the virtual exclusion of ourselves. Vague references to 'rational' inferences have substituted for a proper discussion of the role of human agency. For us, therefore, the utility of Kuhn's comprehensive discussion of research is in setting this imbalance to rights: our particular interest must be in the social-psychological dimension in Kuhn's account. With this in mind let us turn first to Kuhn's early work on scientific discovery.

A discovery is something uncovered, revealed, made visible for the first time. Unlike an invention, which we must construct, a discovery is fully preconstituted and is simply encountered; hence invention is a process but discovery an event. What is discovered is all there already. A discovery is wholly of the world. One cannot discover untruths, since nothing in reality corresponds to them.

At one time this concept of discovery figured prominently in the history of science. The growth of knowledge was conceived of as a series of discoveries. Each event in the series added another permanent component to the growing stockpile of knowledge. And each event was simply an encounter between an individual and an aspect of reality. The individual was, as it were, a camera, recording truth as a film records an image. His previous socialisation was either harmful or at best irrelevant to his task, just as pre-exposing a film generally harms and never helps its performance. Openness to experience and the capacity for rational inference were all that was required of him, just as an aperture and a lens free of aberrations are all that is required of a camera. In short, the concept of discovery was part of a scheme of interpretation which related scientific knowledge entirely to nature and not at all to culture.

In 'The Historical Structure of Scientific Discovery' (1962) Kuhn criticises this concept of discovery by analysing concrete examples. His main focus is upon the discovery of oxygen gas, an event traditionally identified either with an experiment carried out by Priestley in 1775, or another executed by Lavoisier in 1776. Kuhn, however, considers the historical record and the concept of discovery in more detail. Is the discoverer of oxygen the first person to obtain a sample of the gas? If this were so, then Hales in the 1730s would be the discoverer, or, failing that, Bayen in the early 1770s. Both did what is required to produce the gas, and both collected the gas thereby produced. But both failed to identify the gas as a new kind of substance. They did not know what they had, and accordingly they have never been recognised as its discoverers. Having a vessel-full of oxygen did not make Hales its discoverer, any more than having a lung-full of it made Adam its discoverer. Possession is not nine-tenths of the law when it comes to discovery; one has to change one's thinking — to know what one is in possession of. Hence, if discovery is an event at all, it must be a psychological event — a new perception, a flash of insight, a change of *gestalt*.

Priestley was one of the first individuals to make oxygen and then become aware that he had something new or unusual. But this awareness grew by degrees. Priestley began by thinking he had prepared a sample of common air, and only slowly came to understand that this was not so. There was no single psychological event, but a drawn-out process of cognitive reorientation.

Moreover, Priestley changed his thinking in the 'wrong' way. He conceived of combustion as emission: burning material gave off a substance called 'phlogiston'. Materials ceased to burn in a given amount of common air because that air became saturated with 'phlogiston' and there was no room for any more. The same materials burned longer and more fiercely in the new gas, and it was this that persuaded Priestley that the gas was a new one. Since it was very like common air in other ways, Priestley conceived of the gas as common air with less than the normal amount of 'phlogiston' already present; it was air which could take up more phlogiston than normal air. Accordingly, Priestley called the new gas 'dephlogisticated air', a term which reflected his 'incorrect' theoretical orientation.

For something closer to 'truth' it is usual to look to Lavoisier. Following Priestley's work, Lavoisier studied 'dephlogisticated air' in 1776. As a result, he gradually modified his preconception that air was a single homogenous kind, and concluded that 'dephlogisticated air' was in fact a separable component of a mixture of gases in common air. He renamed the component 'oxygen gas', the term which remains in use today. 'Oxygen', however, meant 'acid-forming' and reflected a theoretical orientation just as much as did 'dephlogisticated air'. It was, moreover, an orientation every bit as erroneous by current criteria as Priestley's. Lavoisier's 'error' is less perceptible than Priestley's because it has been 'corrected' by a change of meaning in the concept 'oxygen', whereas Priestley's has been commemorated by a change of terminology.

The story could be elaborated and continued, but there is no point. Enough conceptual chaos has been displayed. We have seen a term which denotes a point event employed to refer to drawn-out cognitive processes. And we have seen a term which denotes the production of truth employed to refer to the cognitive processes of past scientists, processes which by present-day criteria almost invariably resulted in error. To make out discovery as a unit event has obvious convenience in science itself: it legitimates the expedient communal decisions which honour selected individual scientists as 'discoverers'. But the same strategy of description does violence to history if the example above is at all typical.

Was the process of cognitive reorientation that was the discovery of oxygen a special case? Was it the consequence of oxygen being an invisible 'theoretical entity' rather than something observable? It is important to be clear that this was not so. Kuhn himself tells a similar story of the discovery of the planet Uranus, and there are various independent accounts of discoveries which corroborate Kuhn's. For example, in a paper which discusses a range of interesting sociological issues, Woolgar (1976) describes the discovery of pulsars by radio-astronomers. Pulsars may be thought of as stars which emit energy in regular pulses, instead of continuously like the stars with which most of us are familiar. It might be thought that their discovery was simply the first event wherein a radio-telescope was pointed at a pulsar and the regular flashes of signal observed. But Woolgar's account confounds any 'event' model.

A blurred smudge was noticed by chance on a number of pen-chart records of a signal derived from a scanning radio-telescope. As a result further recordings were made, and after many vicissitudes charts indicating a regularly varying input signal were produced. Calculations were made, and enquiries initiated, to see whether the signals were terrestrial or celestial in origin. The signals disappeared, then reappeared again. Observations and theoretical calculations continued: to check whether the signals originated within or without the solar system; whether a point source or extended source was involved; and whether spurious effects, due to instrumentation used, were being misinterpreted. Before discovery claims were published, many individuals had been involved, contributing and combining different skills and competences.

Discovering pulsars was a process of cognitive change, initially within a small group of scientists. This is the typical pattern. However clear nature's communications might be, they are not encoded in language: nature does not describe herself. It is we who give meaning to her messages by determining how they should be fitted into existing concepts and beliefs, and how far our existing concepts and beliefs should be modified and extended to accommodate them. Another way of putting this is to say that there is no relevant difference between 'theoretical' and 'factual' concepts in science: both kinds of concept are our *inventions* — 'star' and 'pulsar' as much as 'phlogiston' and 'oxygen'. And from this it follows that to 'discover' corresponding entities of either kind involves processes of cognitive reorientation.

What, however, if nature merely confirms our pre-existing theories? What if a community is cognitively fully prepared for a discovery before it is made? Cannot such discoveries be made more or less instantaneously, in contrast to the *unanticipated* discoveries discussed above which required cognitive reorientation? This is indeed Kuhn's position in his 1962 paper, but it is too conservative.

Consider Woolgar's account of the pulsar discovery. Would it have had any more of the character of an event if it had been predicted in advance, so that the observations were merely taken as routine confirmations of existing theory? Surely a series of observations and calculations would still have been compiled; alternative hypotheses would still have been eliminated; apparatus would still have been checked over. All this would have been necessary, if only to *validate* the discovery. But the term 'discovery' is used precisely to denote a validated finding; groundless speculations and uncontrolled or unconfirmed observations are never called 'discoveries', because they involve no component of validation. The very activity of making a discovery is presumed to involve ascertainment that what is being discovered is truly what it is. 'Discovery' is a social category of approbation denoting the validated status of that to which it refers (Brannigan, forthcoming). To say that something is a discovery is to describe it as the outcome of a procedure which at once records and validates it. But it is also, as we have seen, to imply that the procedure in question is encompassed within a single act or event. Hence use of the term 'discovery' implies that validation can be accomplished as one event, truly a sign of an inadequate theory of knowledge.

There is no disentangling 'discovery' from the associated epistemology; the term is irredeemably bound up with it. Accordingly, Kuhn's recommendation of two decades ago, that discovery be understood as process rather than event, is unduly cautious; it is more profitable to abandon serious use of the term altogether. To speak of 'discovery' is to abet a form of collective self-forgetfulness, harmless, even 'functional', in science itself, but disastrous if the aim is to study science (cf. also section 5.1).

3.2 Normal Science

Let us now examine Kuhn's own account of research. His focus is upon a group of scientists, united in its use of some existing problem-solution(s) or paradigm(s). This specific kind of consensus is the basis of *normal science*, the typical mode of operation of a scientific community, and the mode for which the training already described serves as appropriate preparation. The advent of normal science marks the coming of age of a scientific field, the point at which really effective, productive research begins. All recognised sciences have passed such a watershed, and it can be queried whether those subjects which have yet to do so deserve to be called sciences at all (Kuhn, 1970, ch. 2). In any case, normal, paradigm-based, scientific research is the point of departure for Kuhn's own discussion, and its character must be understood if the general implications of that discussion are to be grasped.

It is easy to see that agreement upon a paradigm can improve communication in a community, and hence the over-all coherence and efficiency of its research. Nor is there any need to describe how it can restrict speculation and close options. But how does accep-tance of a paradigm indicate problems for research; and how does a paradigm itself actually serve as a resource for the scientist? Curiously, the answer lies in the perceived inadequacy of a para-digm as it is initially formulated and accepted, in its crudity, its unsatisfactory predictive power, and its limited scope, which may in some cases amount to but a single application. In agreeing upon a paradigm scientists do not accept a finished product: rather, they agree to accept a basis for future work, and to treat as illusory or eliminable all its apparent inadequacies and defects. Paradigms are refined and elaborated in normal science. And they are used in the development of further problem-solutions, thus extending the scope of scientific competences and procedures. Where such attempts at elaboration and development fail, the result is a failure for the scientist. His apparatus, his competence or his fortune must take the blame, for to blame the paradigm itself is to initiate a break with normal science.

Normal science is thus a process of extending and filling out the realm of the known; it does not look for fundamental novelties. None the less it is far from being the kind of heavily routinised and intellectually empty drudgery that some commentators have assumed. The tasks of normal science vary enormously, and even the most mundane of them can be immensely challenging. No part of normal science is less demanding than the observation and measurement of those quantities given significance by paradigms. Think of specific gravities, specific heats, conductivities or contact potentials in physics, or atomic weights in chemistry. When the acceptance of a paradigm first establishes the importance of such a quantity, it is typically known in but a few instances, and inexactly and unreliably known in those. There is a felt need to improve techniques of measurement, and to extend them to more cases. Some of this work is indeed undemanding, to the extent that scientists themselves set little store by it and leave others to carry it out. But even here real intellectual and technical challenges do arise. To improve the accuracy of a measurement is a theoretical problem as much as a technical one. It involves considering all possible sources of error in an apparatus and set of procedures, and thus all possible sources of disturbance of ideal measurement conditions. This in turn involves a theoretical orientation to the physical environment — the forces and fields present in it, the sources of local variation in the forces and fields, the underlying nature of the materials from which the apparatus is made, and so on without obvious end. Thus, even at the most everyday level of normal science, theory and practice run together, and intellectual demands continue to arise.

At the other extreme are problems which make obvious and far-reaching demands upon the intellect and the imagination. These involve the construction of new problem-solutions by analogy with existing ones, or, to put the same thing in another way, the reconstruction of existing problem-solutions so that they fit new situations. A new situation has to be creatively reconstructed, and thereby perceived, as *like* a known problem-solution: inference has to proceed analogically from one concrete case to another. This kind of development has been beautifully described by Truesdell (1967) in the growth of mechanics, and Kuhn (1970, p. 190) takes his own illustration of the process from the same context: he discusses the solution to the problem of the motion of the point-mass pendulum, and the story of its subsequent exploitation (cf. Figure 3.1).

In brief, the motion of a mass concentrated at a single point, swinging freely at the end of a weightless thread of constant length, became a solved problem early in the history of mechanics. Galileo had obtained both that and the associated motion of a ball rolling down an inclined plane. He recognised that the key variables in both cases were height and speed; he knew how they were related; and he knew the specially simple conditions at the extreme points of motion, where speed became zero as height came to its maximum, and then speed reached its maximum value as the point of least height was passed through. To Galileo the two motions (parts a and

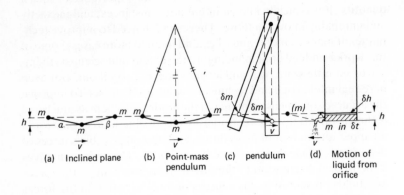

FIGURE 3.1   *The use of a paradigm example*

b in the figure) were relevantly analogous.

Once obtained, the problem-solution of the point-mass pendulum offered a basis for the computation of the motions of other pendula, and indeed of any other motions that could be seen as relevantly analogous to it: the problem-solution became a paradigm. It is easy to see how a real pendulum made of a light string and a very dense mass could be treated as an approximation of the point-mass pendulum. More profoundly, Huygens used the paradigm to obtain the motion of any real pendulum or swinging extended mass (such as, for example, a ruler swinging from one end). The extended mass had to be analysed into a large number of point-masses, so that the tendencies of all the point-masses could be combined to yield information about the behaviour of the whole. (Cf. part c in the figure.) It is easy to recognise this approach continuing in use in methods which employ the calculus to determine the centre of gravity of a body, and then treat the body as a point-mass located at that centre of gravity. These widely used methods exploit a mathematical technique to extend the scope of paradigms based on the idealisation of the point-mass. Finally, Kuhn notes how Daniel Bernoulli perceived the paradigm form in the unsolved problem of the flow of water from an orifice in a tank. Particles of water leaving the orifice in an instant of time must possess sufficient speed to carry them to a height which exactly balances the loss of height of the water within the vessel in the same time (see part d in the figure).

The central point in this example is that the scientist must actively construct an analogy between the known and the unknown, in order to understand and explain the latter. The paradigm is a resource for the scientist, not a determinant of what he does. Paradigms are not algorithms. They cannot instruct the scientist how to carry out his research; they merely remain available as resources for use in that research. Like accepted judicial decisions, they provide precedents to be further specified and articulated (Kuhn, 1970, p. 23). Nothing is deducible from them. Rather than deducing a problem-solution from another more general one, or from an abstract theory, the scientist has actively to make his problem visible and tractable as the same as an existing paradigm. He has to *make* the unknown into an instance of the known, into another routine case.

Let us supplement Kuhn's example with something which illustrates the essential point more simply, at the cost of being hypothetical and unconnected with the history of science. Suppose we know that the area of a triangle is ½ x length of base x length of perpendicular from base to opposite vertex — i.e. ½ x BC x AD in Figure 3.2(a). Suppose also that the area of a parallelogram (in part b) is unknown. There is no way in which the paradigm (a) tells anyone how to solve the problem (b). But a construction makes (a) utilisable in the solution of (b). If *we* add a diagonal, as in (c), the parallelogram can be dealt with as two triangles, and its area calculated as

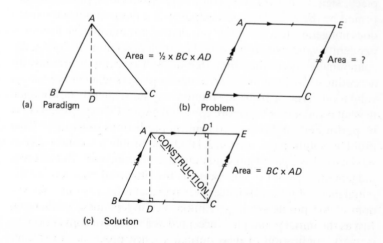

(a) Paradigm

(b) Problem

(c) Solution

FIGURE 3.2   *A paradigm as a resource*

$2 \times \frac{1}{2} \times BC \times AD = BC \times AD$. Making the construction facilitates a direct move from one problem-solution to another.

In summary, then, normal science involves extending and developing the known; but the process is not a formal or deductive one. Nor is it a matter of following instructions or rules. Rather, normal science is a test of ingenuity and imagination, with paradigms figuring large among the cultural resources of the scientist. Success and failure are conventionally taken as indicators of skill in research: the former may enhance the credibility of a paradigm, but the latter does not count against it. Kuhn neatly combines all these themes when he describes normal science as *puzzle-solving*, and makes an analogy with crosswords, jigsaws, chess problems and the like (1970, pp. 36–9). Consider a chess problem. It generally has a unique solution; but this cannot be deduced. Both existing knowledge and ingenuity in its use are required, and both are obtained by practising problem-solving and becoming familiar with existing problem-solutions. The skilled problem-solver sees the themes of solved problems in those he seeks to solve. He takes the former as resources for the imagination, and the latter as tests of his knowledge and his cognitive adroitness.

There is one way in which the analogy with puzzles could possibly mislead. Sometimes, when a puzzle is completed, an independent indication of validity is available. A jigsaw, on insertion of the final piece, signals its own completion; the crossword's validity is confirmed by the next day's newspaper. But a piece of normal science does not generate a candidate problem-solution which is then independently validated. If the way the problem-solution is obtained is communally acceptable, then that in itself constitutes grounds for accepting it. Normal science is at once a process of invention and of validation. True, a problem-solution may subsequently be obtained in what is judged to be a more convincing way. Or experiments may be performed, and judged to confirm predictions suggested by the problem-solution (cf. section 2.1). Or the problem-solution may itself be used as a paradigm, and judged to function well. But all these judgements are of the same kind as that involved in accepting the initial piece of normal science: they represent the conventional wisdom of the puzzle-solving tradition, not independent evaluation. Just as the initial paradigm is accepted as a matter of convention, so is every application of it as normal science proceeds. In science there is no equivalent of the next day's newspaper: there is no basis for validation superior to the collective contingent judgement of the paradigm-sharing community itself.

Current sociological work relies heavily upon Kuhn's account of normal science, and takes much of it for granted. Most writers recognise the importance of communal consensus in research, and the role of the knowledge and competence received from the ancestors. Some are willing to go further and accept that judgement and evaluation in normal science is accurately described; and those who deny this none the less recognise the importance of the questions of validity raised by Kuhn's work. But the sociological literature has still fully to come to terms with Kuhn's account of the role of the accepted problem-solution. Let us consider why Kuhn lays so much stress upon paradigms, and, in comparison with other writers, so little upon verbal rules and generalisations, or symbolic laws.

Kuhn initially justifies his stress upon paradigms by straightforward appeal to experience. A large part of the history of science is manifestly visible, as far as Kuhn is concerned, as paradigm-based research. Similarly, he sees present-day science education as a training in the use of accepted problem-solutions. And when he reviews his own experience of actual scientific communities, he finds that they possess nothing like a sufficient number of rules and generalisations to account for research practice. Moreover, scientists working closely together within a single research tradition are often unable to agree which precise rules and principles guide their work, whereas they immediately cite the same central problem-solutions and concrete models. Accordingly, all the evidence points to the priority of paradigms. Paradigms suffice as a basis for research; and it is empirically evident that scientists use them in preference to rules (Kuhn, 1970, ch. 5).

paradigms rather than rules as the basis of research.

There is, however, a more radical conclusion which Kuhn's discussion can help us towards, and which ties in very closely with themes already discussed in the previous chapter. If research is based upon verbal rules and principles rather than paradigms, then how the terms in the rules relate to nature must be clear. *But establishing this relationship is the very function which Kuhn attributes to paradigms.* If the general thrust of Kuhn's account is correct, then without concrete examples, and hence, in physical science, without paradigms, there can be no understanding at all of the proper usage of scientific terms; how such terms apply in specific cases cannot be deduced from their abstract presentation in laws and theories (cf.

paradigms fix application of scientific terms

also section 2.2). Hence it is not so much that scientists have chosen to base research on paradigms as that science must proceed on the basis of paradigms. Paradigms are to concepts like 'mass' and 'force' what concrete instances are to concepts like 'cat' or 'shirt'.

This relationship of paradigms and concepts is stressed many times in Kuhn's work. Yet the notion that rules and paradigms are separable components in research, each capable of guiding investigation independently, is never fully abandoned. The impossibility of replacing paradigms with rules is never made clear; Kuhn merely argues that it is undesirable (cf. 1974, pp. 313–19). Perhaps this over-conservative position is connected with Kuhn's evaluative concerns. He regards paradigms as the distinctively valuable components of scientific culture. But if science is *demarcated* from other viable forms of culture by use of paradigms instead of rules, then rules must provide a viable alternative to paradigms.

Once it is recognised that the concepts of the physical sciences must be keyed into nature by way of paradigms and particular applications, an illuminating equivalence is immediately evident between training and research. In training, the scientist learns the accepted similarity relations by exposure to successive particular instances, or applications, of terms. He is judged competent when his subsequent development of similarity relations runs along the lines accepted in his community; this is indicated by the way he solves routine problems not completely familiar to him but familiar to his teachers. In research, the scientist solves problems by modelling them on existing solved problems or paradigms; and he thus again develops similarity relations to cover further cases. The difference is that this time the cases are as unfamiliar to the community as to him, and he must hope that the community comes to accept his work as sound. As far as cognitive processes themselves are concerned, there is no fundamental difference between learning and innovating in the context of normal science. And this is precisely why the learning process described by Kuhn (see Chapter 2) is such an effective and appropriate preparation for research.

Training displays similarity relations by linking instances to instances; research extends similarity relations by linking instances to instances. The links are made in both cases by analogy. In training one learns how to see a problem in terms of a known one, and thus how to calculate values for variables in the problem. Exactly the same happens in research. By seeing the unknown in terms of a known problem-solution, inductive inference is possible: variables in the unknown situation are calculated by assuming that it behaves analogously to a known one. Thus science proceeds by analogy and induction, with the former licensing the latter. Where analogy is perceived, expectation is projected. In training, the perceptual and cognitive processes whereby analogy is perceived are socialised until analogies in standard situations are projected along acceptable lines; in research, these socialised processes project analogies in less standardised circumstances.

Although scientists often assume that their concepts and theories in some sense already apply through the whole of nature, what they effectively do in the course of normal research is actively to arrange phenomena under concepts, instance by instance. It is the activity of normal science that gives concepts significance, not the inherent significance of concepts that determines the activity. Thus in Kuhn's description of normal science we have a *finitist* account of concept application of the kind discussed in section 2.3 above. In one way, however, it is a better account, for it reveals how scientists, in modelling one situation upon another, construct, as much as perceive, the resemblances in question.

3.3 Scientific revolutions

The group of scientists trained for normal research is at the same time a sensitive detector of anomaly. A strong set of expectations throws into relief whatever fails to confirm them, any puzzle which resists solution, any phenomenon which defies analysis as the familiar in unfamiliar form. Moreover, since scientists often manifest an intense and exclusive commitment to their paradigms (see section 2.1), and may even insist upon an ontology containing only paradigmatic entities or processes, anomalies are often focused upon as things with no right to exist, insults to orthodox doctrine.

Hence much normal research tends to focus upon anomaly. Puzzle-solving activity frequently attempts to show that what is *prima facie* anomalous is either the spurious product of bad equipment or technique, or a familiar phenomenon in disguise. And most anomalies are successfully assimilated in this way. Some, however, stubbornly persist, and become widely known as vexatious problems. Over time, these recalcitrant anomalies accumulate as the by-products of normal research; and they can in some circumstances generate a malaise, or even a sense of crisis, among practitioners. The existence of an accumulating residue of problems which persistently resists all attempts at assimilation may, according to Kuhn, at last prompt the widespread suspicion that something is at fault at the heart of normal research itself.

The response to a crisis of this kind typically involves a change in the character of research. Speculation becomes more acceptable. Novel and radically deviant procedures and interpretations are tried. Paradigms, and the activities and judgements based upon them, are called into question. They are not, however, discarded: no scientific community ever simply throws aside its tools and abandons research. Only when a new paradigm is agreed upon, as an adequate response to current difficulties and an acceptable foundation for future work, only then can the existing basis for research be set on one side. At this point a large scale re-ordering of practice and perception occurs, reflecting the requirements exemplified in the new paradigm; and the conceptual fabric undergoes an analogous reconstruction. The scene is now set for a new sequence of normal science to develop: a *scientific revolution* has occurred.

Among Kuhn's examples of scientific revolutions are those which occurred, in chemistry, with the acceptance of the oxygen theory of combustion and, later, of Daltonian atomism, in physics, at the transition from Aristotelian to classical mechanics, and then again with the advent of quantum mechanics and relativistic mechanics, and in astronomy, with the acceptance of the Copernican system. He also cites 'lesser' revolutions such as those associated with the discoveries of X-radiation and the planet Uranus (cf. Kuhn, 1970, chs 8–10).

In general, Kuhn expects to find normal research interrupted by revolutionary episodes. At times of revolution scientists make the drastic responses necessary to cope with accumulating anomaly, but quite impracticable in the context of the normal science which produced it. Revolutions are to be expected because they perform an essential function; they are vital to the evolution of scientific culture, just as they are vital to the evolution of political institutions (cf. Kuhn, 1970, ch. 9). Here, as everywhere, Kuhn writes as a functionalist; and his account will only be acceptable exactly as it stands to those who see no difficulties in the functionalist point of view.

Kuhn goes out of his way to emphasise that revolutions constitute discontinuities in research and the growth of knowledge. By reconstructing it around a new achievement scientists effect a truly radical transformation of their culture, at the verbal and symbolic level as well as at the level of procedure and perception. Learned similarity relations are modified, with concrete instances being grouped into new clusters: before Dalton the alloys of the metals were compounds; after his work they were mixtures; in mechanics before Newton, terrestrial and celestial objects were fundamentally different; after his work they were mechanically identical. The conceptual fabric is also reconstructed so that concepts figure in different laws and generalisations; this happened with the term 'compound' as a result of Dalton's work, and to 'mass' as a result of Einstein's. Thus, if we examine a scientific field before and after a revolution, we observe what are essentially two distinct ways of life, maintaining two distinct systems of verbal culture. The reconstruction of practice results in new modes of cognition, inference and explanation; sometimes these amount to a new world-view, which is transmitted by authority to new generations of scientists just as was the world-view it replaced.

This discontinuity in practice, language and perception is, Kuhn stresses, also a discontinuity in scientific judgement. The basis for the evaluation of knowledge-claims is different after a revolution. Nor is the decision to change paradigms ever compelled by the indications of logic and experiment alone: paradigms are formally *incommensurable*. Although Kuhn believes that a specific set of perceived anomalies precipitates a scientific revolution, and that most scientists find these anomalies better accounted for on the basis of the new paradigm, he takes these as contingent facts, solely of social-psychological interest. They do not prove, nor could there be a proof, that the new paradigm is intrinsically the better, or even that any reasonable person at the time would be compelled to accept it as the better. In the last analysis there is no way of ranking paradigms and their associated conceptual fabrics according to their intrinsic merit as determined by logic and experiment alone. Nor is there any clear sense in which a later paradigm and conceptual fabric is ontologically superior to an earlier one.

It was this account of scientific revolutions, with its explicit relativistic implications, which ensured that Kuhn's work became widely known. Normal science was not so arresting a phenomenon, and some commentators, noting Kuhn's own references to its 'cumulative' character, even managed to interpret it as nothing more than 'rational enquiry' in the traditional sense. The consequent image of revolutions as impassable crevasses ripping across the path of rational scientific progress was vivid and exciting, and aroused great interest. This was, however, an image sustained entirely by an outmoded and untenable stereotype of the growth of knowledge; and when it is set aside the value of Kuhn's concept becomes more open to question, and several weaknesses become evident in the manner of its formulation.

Few commentators would deny that the empirical characteristics of scientific revolutions are inadequately specified in Kuhn's *Structure*; and the lack of any development in this regard in the two subsequent decades greatly adds to the force of the criticism. Revolutions range from massive reconstructions extending over decades, to quickly accomplished cognitive and procedural reorientations such as are implied, for example, by the discovery of a new planet. They include changes in the common culture of the educated elite of the whole of Europe, and esoteric modifications in the accepted problem-solutions of small groups of highly specialised professionals. They are generally defined as retooling operations with important consequences for research practice, but they are occasionally treated more abstractly as changes in cosmology or worldview. One is bound to wonder why Kuhn has never sought to prune and discipline this initial diversity of sense.

The story of how revolutions arise and proceed is more satisfactory, as far as clarity and consistency are concerned. Revolutions are responses to problems within traditions of research, not to external disturbances. They pivot around an accumulated cluster of recalcitrant anomalies. They are carried through by argument and appeal to nature — even if the power of the arguments and appeals is more social-psychological than logical in the accepted sense. The question here is whether Kuhn's account is accurate and sufficient, something which only the collective wisdom of historians will be able to decide. Fortunately, they are well placed to do so over the long term, since Kuhn cites many instances of revolutions which can be considered empirically. For what it is worth, my own reading of current historical research is that it is revealing what are at least significant insufficiencies in Kuhn's account (cf. Chapter 5), though no doubt his characterisation of revolutionary episodes will continue to retain some utility in descriptive historical writing.

Finally, there is the matter of the necessity of scientific revolutions. Kuhn, as we have seen, imbues the alternation of normal and revolutionary science with functional necessity (1970, ch. 9). Commentators accordingly describe his work as a 'theory of scientific development'; and they accept the implication that every episode in the history of an established science must be either 'normal' or 'revolutionary'. This, however, even if it is a legitimate interpretation, is one which demands too much of Kuhn's account. One of the merits of his own properly detailed historical treatment of the Copernican revolution is its demonstration that the changes involved were not necessitated by accumulating anomalies and a sense of crisis: this does not have to be inferred, since it is spelled out in Kuhn's own commentary (Kuhn, 1957, cf. especially ch. 4). That scientific revolutions are functionally necessary is a claim difficult to reconcile with Kuhn's own work, let alone with the full richness of the historical record. It is a claim, moreover, which is offensive to the imagination: it is easy to visualise different kinds of transition from one paradigm and conceptual fabric to another, or even processes which lead to alternative paradigms coexisting alongside each other; nor have we any arguments to suggest that such transitions and processes could not actually occur (cf. also section 4.3).

It is because of its comparative lack of theoretical interest that Kuhn's account of revolutions is less valuable than his discussion of normal science. The latter is of *fundamental* theoretical importance because it describes many general characteristics of cognition and culture which it is difficult to imagine could be otherwise. The former does not do this, and accordingly can be at best no more than an empirical description of some selected episodes in the history of science.

Those parts of *Structure* which describe scientific revolutions are, however, of interest for another reason. They serve as the occasion for an extended discussion of problems of evaluation in science. The difficulties encountered in the comparative appraisal of alternative paradigms and conceptual fabrics are carefully analysed and illustrated, so that the grounds for a relativistic conception of knowledge emerge with striking clarity. A discussion of this more abstract component in Kuhn's treatment of scientific revolutions follows in the next chapter.

3.4   Kuhn's critics

Most of the critical commentaries upon Kuhn are the work of professional epistemologists, and reflect, usually negatively, upon his philosophical significance. These commentaries are none the less widely known and influential within the social sciences, where great importance is attached to the epistemological literature, and in particular to the so-called Popper–Kuhn debate. Any appraisal of the sociological significance of Kuhn's description of science is bound to make an assessment of this material. In what follows I suggest that the material is not in fact of fundamental sociological interest, and that there is considerable confusion over the extent of its relevance to sociological aims and objectives. Since the discussion must necessarily be very brief, I make no attempt to prove my case or to come to terms with specific arguments; I concentrate instead upon making visible those general features of the critical literature which I believe mainly to be responsible for the confusion.

A good way of understanding the orientation of epistemologists is to examine the seven appraisals of Kuhn published as *Criticism and the Growth of Knowledge* (Lakatos and Musgrave, 1970). Five of these essays are by philosophers; two are not. The systematic difference between the five and the two is immediately recognisable. For the latter, the question is whether Kuhn has produced a correct empirical description of science, actual science as we know it. Margaret Masterman thinks that he has, and explains why in an outstandingly useful essay. L. Pearce Williams doubts that he has, and justifies his reserve by pointing to the lack of properly detailed empirical evidence for his general claims (cf. also Pearce Williams, 1980). Inadequate documentation of events in actual science worries the professional historian Pearce Williams, just as subjective observations of actual science convince the scientist Masterman. In contrast, none of the five philosophical criticisms give major significance to empirical findings, and some disdain them. Popper himself actually finds Pearce Williams's call for empirical evidence 'surprising and disappointing' (1970, pp. 57–8).

The criticisms of the philosophers are not, in the last analysis, empirically based at all. Activities such as Kuhn describes may, indeed do, exist (cf. Lakatos and Musgrave, 1970, pp. 25, 52). But such activities do not *deserve* to be called scientific, even if they actually are so called. Mere actuality is no more than a side issue.

The philosophers *stipulate* what science is, and, when forced to choose between common usage and their stipulations, fall back on the latter. Thus, ultimately, for a Popperian, science is what Popperian philosophy asserts it to be, and not necessarily what is typically encountered in accepted scientific contexts. Should the world's scientific manpower turn (or turn out to be) Kuhnian or Baconian, it would be said that they had abandoned science.

Most epistemologists and all Popperians have a normative orientation to science, not a naturalistic one. They aspire to be moralists. They moralise with the term 'science' and about science. Accordingly, they tend to read Kuhn as a moralist also, and they dislike what they read. Kuhn does not make a satisfactory demarcation between science and non-science; indeed, his work undermines any such demarcation, and consequently frustrates the grand undertaking of separating 'reason' from 'unreason'. If there are scientific revolutions, Lakatos points out, then the growth of knowledge is insufficiently determined by 'rules of reason'; it is thus open to 'religious maniacs' to justify their irrationalism by pointing to its existence in science itself (1970, p. 93). Similarly, if normal science exists, then it is well nigh impossible to demarcate scientific from customary activity. Therefore, normal science must not exist. What Kuhn refers to by the term must be redefined as unscientific:

> the condition which Kuhn regards as the normal and proper condition of science is a condition which, if it actually obtained, Popper would regard as *un*scientific (Watkins, 1970, p. 28).

> [what Kuhn describes as normal science] is a phenomenon which I dislike (because I regard it as a danger to science) while he apparently does not dislike it (because he regards it as 'normal') (Popper, 1970, p. 52).

> *Belief* may be a regrettably unavoidable biological weakness to be kept under the control of criticism: but *commitment* is for Popper an outright crime.
> Kuhn thinks otherwise (Lakatos, 1970, p. 92).

Kuhn, then, is read as a moralist, and criticised for advocating the wrong things. Nor is this an altogether implausible reading. Being neither epistemologist nor sociologist Kuhn can and does allow himself the luxury of being normative and descriptive simultaneously. In his own essay in *Criticism and the Growth of Knowledge* he recognises this, and explicitly sets out how he relates these two dimensions of his thinking:

> The structure of my argument is simple and, I think, unexceptionable: scientists behave in the following ways; those modes of behaviour have (here theory enters) the following essential functions; in the absence of an alternate mode *that would serve similar functions*, scientists should behave essentially as they do if their concern is to improve scientific knowledge (in Lakatos and Musgrave, 1970, p. 237).

This is moralising of a much more modest kind than that of the Popperians. And, crucially, it places empirical study prior to normative concerns: independent knowledge of actual science is necessary, whether one's eventual goal is descriptive or normative. Kuhn draws normative conclusions only after he has undertaken an empirically informed account of how science actually proceeds; and this is what makes his work empirically and hence sociologically interesting. In much epistemological writing, on the other hand, normative considerations run through everything, and frequently become intertwined with empirical claims in a very seriously misleading way (cf. Law, 1975; Barnes, 1976).

Popperian epistemology has fundamentally the character of a moral code; it has no sociological interest as an account of science. This in itself is no cause for condemnation. Everybody moralises: there are no exceptions. But if moralising is an unavoidable biological weakness, conflating it with description is an outright crime — a crime which, knowingly or unknowingly, the Popperians frequently commit. Consequently, it is all too easy to mistake the impossible (and undesirable) prescriptions of Popperian epistemology for a well-informed exposition of the features of actual science.

For example, although the empirical study of actual science is something which most Popperian epistemologists set little store by, they none the less cite that actuality against Kuhn. The impression is created that not only is Kuhn a man of dubious morals, but that he does not know much about actual science either. This impression is, however, the result of an oscillation between prescriptive and descriptive orientations. Empirical evidence which supports Kuhn is made out as irrelevant, since it is by stipulation not genuine science that is involved; empirical evidence which supports a Popperian view is cited as it stands. The Popperian critique is thus bound to succeed whatever the empirical state of affairs. Despite innumerable references to Galileo and Newton, Einstein and Bohr, all that Popperian criticism expresses is a rejection of Kuhn's image of how science should be, and a dogmatic assertion of Popper's.

It is important that the empirical emptiness of such criticism is clearly understood, lest it give a false impression of the nature of science as it is actually practised. Unfortunately, its authors are less than helpful here. It is not just that they conflate description and prescription. Sometimes they appear to believe that their fancies as to what science should be can actually influence how it is. They project the outcome of their moralising into the world, and see it as a force making its mark upon history.

Take, for example, the contribution of Imre Lakatos, in which is presented a *philosophical* theory of scientific growth. The gist of Lakatos's theory is that science grows under the impetus of competing research programmes which from time to time undergo 'progressive' or 'degenerative' problem shifts: the rational preference of scientists for programmes where 'progressive' rather than 'degenerative' shifts occur results in scientific progress.

Historians have sometimes mistaken this for an *empirical* theory, and have attempted to test it against concrete historical materials, or to compare it with supposedly competing accounts like Kuhn's (Gay, 1976; Frankel, 1979). What it actually involves, however, is the transposition of an empirical description — that of Kuhn — so that it no longer refers to the empirical realm. To quote Lakatos: 'my concept of a "research programme" may be construed as an objective, "third world" reconstruction of Kuhn's socio-psychological concept of paradigm' (1970, p. 179). Theories of the 'third world' apply to an independent realm of ideas, 'Plato's and Popper's "third world"' (1970, p. 180), wherein there occurs, not the growth of actual science, but the growth of a 'rationally-reconstructed' science (1970, p. 179).

Lakatos's 'theory of scientific growth' applies to a 'rationally-reconstructed' history of science. How, then, is this produced? The answer completes a circle: history must be rewritten so that it accords with Lakatos's theory — no matter that this involves writing false history, since the falsehoods will be the history of science as it should have been (cf. 1970, pp. 138ff). Given this, it is scarcely to be wondered at that Lakatos's theory applies in the 'third world', since this 'third world' is actually designed to be in accord with the theory. It is a Platonic realm conjured into existence precisely to give Popperian epistemology something to refer to.

Secure in its Platonic realm, Lakatos's account is immune to the findings of actual history. Hence one might reasonably imagine that if it is of any relevance at all it is at least not of empirical relevance. This, however, is not Lakatos's view. The history of the third world, the false history which projects Lakatos's fancy for how science should have been, evidently has consequences for what exists in actual history:

> the mirror image of the third world in the mind of the individual — even in the mind of the 'normal' — scientists is usually a caricature of the original; and to describe this caricature without relating it to the third-world original might well result in a caricature of a caricature. One cannot understand the history of science without taking into account the interaction of the three worlds (Lakatos, 1970, p. 180).

Having produced an account of science in the 'third world' which he acknowledges to be a reconstruction modelled on Kuhn's account of actual science, Lakatos criticises Kuhn for ignoring this 'third-world original'. But neither in this contribution nor in his later developments of his ideas does Lakatos show how reference to such an 'original' can be reconciled with reputable historical practice.

Empirical findings cannot help force a decision between Lakatos and Kuhn, and those historians who have sought to use them thus have, at best, been wasting their time. Anything which supports Kuhn will either support Lakatos equally well, or will be unfit for admittance to the Platonic realm. Anything which goes against Kuhn can always be so reconstructed *en route* to the Platonic realm that it supports Lakatos on arrival. Historians cannot give concrete support to Lakatos's theory: in seeking to do so they treat a philosophical theory of the Platonic realm as if it were the empirical, falsifiable, kind of scientific theory described in the early writings of Popper himself, before he turned to Platonism. Lakatos's theory needs no empirical support. Its acceptance simply involves acceptance of Lakatos's values, acceptance of the Platonism which allows their representation as an independent realm of ideas, and acceptance of the parapsychological conjecture that in their manifestation as independent ideas his values interact with the minds of other men. A historian who uses Lakatos's theory must cease to be a historian, and adopt instead the methods of 'rational reconstruction' (cf. Lakatos, 1970, p. 138, and especially note 2). It is fascinating to compare these methods, involving as they do both extremes of Whiggism and the wilful distortion of events, with the properly historical procedures used by Kuhn and outlined in Chapter 1 above. There can surely be little doubt that once historians correctly understand the demands made by Lakatos's philosophical theory, they will lose any inclination to minister to them.

In general, the normative concerns common among epistemologists are difficult to reconcile with an empirical orientation to science. Admittedly, I have illustrated this point with an extreme example. Few epistemologists are such enthusiasts as those of the Popperian school, and even fewer allow their enthusiasms such latitude. Not all epistemologists believe, as one Popperian evidently does, that to do science is to 'participate in the divine'; nor, I suspect, do all of them feel 'awe at the transcendental miracle of mathematics and science' (Jarvie, 1979, p. 496). There is much to be learned from epistemologists who are willing to let a matter-of-fact approach predominate in their thinking, and from those such as Quine who somehow manage to assert their values without destroying the empirical relevance of their work. None the less the epistemological literature has always to be addressed with great care, and indeed suspicion, by anyone with empirical objectives. Sociology, like history, is concerned with the empirical understanding of what is generally taken to be science. The first question sociologists must ask of Kuhn's work is precisely Pearce Williams's question, which so surprised and disappointed Popper: is actual science as Kuhn describes it?

4

Evaluation

4.1 Alternative paradigms

Much has already been said about the evaluation of knowledge, since it is part and parcel of the research process and not a separate mode of activity. The grounds for treating evaluation as inexplicable simply by reference to logic and experience have already been indicated. None the less a more abstract discussion may be helpful in establishing this controversial assessment of what is possible in the way of evaluation in science. And the basis for such a discussion is provided in Kuhn's *Structure*.

That judgements made in the course of normal science are culturally specific and conventionally based is clear enough from Kuhn's account (at least it should be; see, however, section 4.3). Such judgements are extensions of custom, which rely upon and affirm the body of accepted doctrine; an autonomous, unconditioned 'reason', whatever that might be, has no role to play in judgements of this kind. Hence, if there is a role for 'reason', it must be at times of paradigm change, when custom to an extent breaks down and the form and relevance of a sociological account of evaluation is less obvious. It is in revolutionary periods, when a choice between alternative modes of conventional activity is possible, that judgements sufficiently determined by logic and experience should appear, if at all. Kuhn, however, shows that they do not appear at such times, and that they cannot.

It is worth noting that if 'reason' could indeed 'break through' at times of scientific revolution, this fact would react back and undermine Kuhn's account of normal science. Research in periods of normal science is based upon commitment to a given paradigm; it is intelligible as a pattern of conventional activity supported by authority and mechanisms of social control. Conflicting paradigms imply conflicting or alternative modes of conventional activity. Clearly the two sets of conventions cannot themselves offer a suitable basis for their own mutual evaluation. But if there were some external factor, 'rationality', or 'reason', *independent of convention*, which could be used to evaluate the alternative conventions, then one would be bound to wonder why it could not enter into normal science itself, and why it could only operate at times of crisis. Acceptance of an independent role for 'reason' would call into question the whole of Kuhn's view of science. Only if reasoning has itself everywhere and always a conventional character can Kuhn's general vision be sustained.

Fortunately, every part of Kuhn's work substantiates the view that reasoning has this character. As far as a decision between paradigms is concerned, logic and experience alone no more suffice than they do in normal science. There is no appropriate scale available with which to weigh the merits of alternative paradigms: they are incommensurable. To favour one paradigm rather than another is in the last analysis to express a preference for one form of life rather than another — a preference which cannot be rationalised by any non-circular argument, as Wittgenstein has shown (1953; cf. Kuhn, 1970, p. 94). But if the insufficiency of 'reason' in the choice between paradigms is best understood by reference to forms of life in precisely Wittgenstein's sense, Kuhn is none the less prepared to discuss it abstractly. He is willing to compare alternative conceptual fabrics, alternative connected systems of concepts and beliefs, in conformity to the idiom of the 'statement view' of scientific theories (cf. Stegmüller, 1976). This part of his discussion has in fact proved a highly successful strategy of communication; it has drawn attention to the significance of his work in a way which his more profound discussion of normal science would not itself have done.

Kuhn's general case against the sufficiency of 'reason' appears in the second half of *Structure* (1970, chs 9, 10, 12). The argument is deceptively informal. Stegmüller (1976, pp. 216ff) dismisses it as a 'bit of musing' by a philosophical incompetent, and suggests that 'experts' will be able to close the 'rationality gaps' which it appears to open. It is noteworthy, however, that Stegmüller himself, a professional epistemologist and virtuoso of set theory, is completely unable to do this. He excuses his failure by suggesting that the field in which he is an expert is 'still in its infancy' (1976, p. 269; cf. also p. 246). But another way of interpreting his failure is as a sign of the soundness and importance of Kuhn's 'bit of musing'.

Dalton
example

Let us consider Kuhn's arguments as he discusses the transition in chemistry from affinity theory to Daltonian atomism (cf. Kuhn, 1970, pp. 130–5). According to the theory of elective affinity, materials were held together by the mutual affinities between their constituent particles or corpuscles. Chemical changes involved realignments of these affinities: copper, for example, would dissolve in a solution of silver in acid, and precipitate the silver, because the affinity of the copper corpuscles for the acid corpuscles was the greater. Such chemical changes were generally accompanied by heat, light, effervescence or some other indication of the vigorous coming together of the corpuscles under the forces of affinity. They resulted in the production of homogeneous materials wherein the independent existence of the constituent combining materials was indiscernible. These materials were chemical *compounds*, and different in kind to the physical mixtures produced without the creation of a truly homogeneous new material. Unlike compounds, mixtures, such as salt and sand, could be separated into their constituents by mechanical means.

Dalton's new theory also described chemical processes in terms of particles (atoms), and also distinguished compounds and mixtures; it was analogous to the earlier theory in a number of ways. But it held in addition that the atoms of any element were all identical with one another, and that chemical combination involved the aggregation of the atoms of different elements in fixed, small, whole-number ratios. This meant that chemical compounds should always contain the same proportions by mass of their constituent elements — a requirement formalised as the Daltonian law of constant composition, and still appearing as such in chemistry curricula.

Why, then, should this significant point of difference between Daltonian atomism and the earlier theory of elective affinity not have been made the basis for a formal comparative evaluation? The two theories made different predictions concerning the composition of compounds, so why should not the results of experiment have arbitrated between them?

Such results, if routinely used, would without doubt have counted against Dalton's position. Affinity theory was largely compatible with experience as conceptualised at the time, but Dalton's theory faced major anomalies. Glasses, metal alloys, minerals and solutions were among entire classes of chemical compounds which clearly departed from the law of constant composition. And even the results which 'confirmed' Dalton did so only upon a charitable interpretation, since chemical analyses never yielded completely identical results from different assays.

However, at the advent of Dalton's theory 'compound' was a similarity relation, a cluster of instances, which had developed alongside affinity theory. The similarity relation and the affinity theory had been constructed as parts of a coherent system of culture: they had been shaped so that they dovetailed together. Hence to test atomism against currently accepted instances of 'compound' was to test it against a reality pre-organised and preconceived in terms of the competing position. Presumably, a man moved solely by 'reason' might properly question the appropriateness of such a test.

There is, however, no way of revising the similarity relation 'compound' so that it provides 'neutral' instances with which to test the alternatives. How would we know which of the endless number of revisions of the conventionally accepted cluster should be taken as 'neutral'?

What happened historically was that as the Daltonian approach gained ground so the similarity relation 'compound' was reconstructed to fit it. Increasingly, Dalton's own law was used to identify compounds: alloys, solutions and the rest were reclassified as mixtures. Culture was resystematised into a new coherent structure. And when this was done, the older view of elective affinity was in the same hopeless position formally as Daltonian atomism had originally been: affinity theory could not account for the manifest invariability of composition in 'compounds', whereas Dalton could.

In actual historical cases, as a new paradigm arises so there is an associated transformation in the entire conceptual fabric. What has to be evaluated are two alternative frameworks of discourse and activity. There is a reconstruction of the whole pattern of both. Terms connect to other terms differently, and they connect to nature differently. Thus after Dalton the term 'compound' came close to being defined by the law of constant composition — a law which had not featured in the earlier conceptual fabric. And 'compound' clustered acids, bases and salts apart from alloys and solutions; it attached to nature differently. Although the sign 'com-

pound' remained in use, the similarity relation 'compound' had
changed. Moreover, the new relation justified the new scientific
laws and generalisations, just as the old relation had justified those
previously held.

It will now be clear that neither the pre- nor the post-Daltonian
conceptual fabrics were of themselves incompatible with
experience, or inconsistent logically. As alternative bases for chemical practice, scientists could assimilate new phenomena to either, in
ways which preserved their utility and coherence. The two alternative conceptual fabrics were the correlates of alternative viable
forms of research: hence Kuhn's claim that no such alternatives can
ever be conclusively measured against each other using only
experience and the resources of deductive logic.

One consequence of Kuhn's stress upon the way similarity
relations, and hence 'meanings', change in revolutions has been an
increased interest in problems of translation. It is sometimes
thought that if the concepts of one conceptual fabric can be unproblematically replaced with those of another, or perhaps the terms of
both with equivalents drawn from some more elaborate and universal set of concepts, then a basis for proper communication, and
(eventually) proper logical evaluation, might after all be displayed
as existing between them. There are very strong grounds for holding
that translation of this kind is not possible (it is, for example, incompatible with the finitist arguments presented in section 2.3); but
even if it were, it would not solve the problem of evaluation which
Kuhn poses.

Where two groups of scientists have become committed to alternative paradigms and conceptual fabrics there are certainly problems of *intelligibility* which may be lessened in practice by attempts
to translate the terms of one fabric into those of the other. Scientists
with different commitments may find that initially they 'talk
through each other', as Kuhn puts is; and attempts at translation
may increase the extent of useful communication, and permit the
exchange of 'persuasive argumentation' in such situations. Thus
attempts at translation may conceivably be of some practical significance in the course of scientific change. But in the last analysis the
best that any translation can do, even in ideal circumstances, is
to produce full and proper awareness of two alternative schemes of
things. The problem of *evaluation* remains (just as it remains in the
example above, where it is hoped that something of both atomism

and affinity theory was communicated to the reader without solving the evaluation problem). The individual scientist must still face the question, as formidable as ever, of which alternative to adopt as the basis of his research. His choice remains that between alternative forms of scientific life.

It is to stress this fact that Kuhn talks of paradigm change requiring 'conversion' of the individual scientist, and a switch of *gestalt*: what is required of a scientific collectivity is something akin to a 'political revolution'. These locutions are well chosen to emphasise the insufficiency of logic and experience alone in deciding between alternative paradigms (cf. Kuhn, 1970, pp. 198–204).

[margin note: conversion gestalt switch political revolution as metaphors.]

Suppose that in a final attempt to evade the implications of Kuhn's account one seeks an *external* standard of evaluation. Atomism and affinity theory cannot be satisfactorily differentiated by their predictions about 'compounds' because the term 'compound' is *internal* to both, and is used differently in the two associated contexts. In the last analysis, translation does not help. But why not seek criteria which involve no internal concepts? Why not, for example, simply compare the number of solved problems achieved by the two alternatives?

Unfortunately, every notion put forward as a basis for 'external' evaluation is itself contestable in its application. What counts as a 'solved problem', for example, is commonly disputed by those committed to alternative paradigms. A Daltonian could perhaps take a 5 per cent variation in analyses of a compound's composition as a successful prediction, while an opponent might take the same variation as an anomaly for atomism: what the first imputed to experimental error and random impurity, the latter might impute to the inherent nature of the compound. Similar difficulties arise if one talks of falsifying instances.

[margin note: what counts as a solved problem varies from paradigm to paradigm so too for falsifying instance]

Terms like 'solved problem', 'falsifying instance' or 'anomaly' do not come with instructions for their proper application. Accordingly, they cannot be applied as the prelude to evaluation by formal, 'purely rational' procedures, as philosophers understand them. The appropriate usage of such terms is capable of being made out in any number of ways, some of which will lend comfort to supporters of one position, and some to supporters of the other. Rather than solving problems of evaluation, the use of such terms merely *creates* new problems of the same kind. Paradigms and their associated conceptual fabrics provide a basis upon which the whole of reality can be constructed, leaving nothing outside themselves as a clearly independent foundation for their evaluation.

Thus Kuhn rebuffs all attempts to decide between atomism and affinity theory by logic and experience alone. And in doing so he accommodates his arguments to those who think in terms of alternative verbal systems competing to explain an unproblematically accepted mass of experience. But, finally, we should remember that pre- and post-Daltonian chemistry were modes of activity, not abstract verbal systems. And both modes were capable of generating and legitimating distinct sets of data. There was no routinely accepted mass of 'experience': what was to count as experience had to be determined by men whose judgements, inferences, perceptions and sensations were liable to be conditioned by their expectations and objectives. It is clear that as Dalton's system spread so the general disposition to accept 'Daltonian' findings increased, as did the proportion of such findings in experimental reports. The database of Daltonian chemists was not an independent realm, but a construction subtly related to their theoretical position (Kuhn, 1970, ch. 10).

These points are vividly conveyed in Kuhn's final and most radical argument for the incommensurability of paradigms. Those committed to alternative paradigms, he says, carry out their research in different worlds (cf. Kuhn, 1970, pp. 111ff). If 'the world' refers not to the physical environment just as it is, unperceived and unverbalised, but to experience and activity, ordered, verbalised, and imbued with significance by a group of men, then Kuhn is indubitably correct in this claim. None the less I wonder whether it is formulated in the most appropriate way. Kuhn's choice of vocabulary here can easily suggest a radically idealist ontology, and a denial of the existence of a single shared physical environment; but there are far too many references to an independent nature throughout his work as a whole for this to stand as a plausible interpretation of his views.

4.2   Conceptual fabrics

Scientific concepts are learned and used in two ways: ostensively, and as components in laws and generalisations. In previous chapters it has only been necessary to consider the former in any detail. But the latter is none the less of crucial importance. If ostension displays instances of concepts, generalisation conveys what we can expect of those instances. If ostension connects concepts to nature, generalisation connects concepts to each other, and makes each one a part of a system of verbal culture. Kuhn's discussion of commensurability and translation in section 4.1 above has already introduced some of the features of such a connected system. In this section, I press the analysis further, concentrating on themes of central sociological interest.

It is always possible to reify the verbal component of a culture as a conceptual fabric, a structure made up of generalisations which connect concepts into a single integrated whole. It is true that something is lost by reducing linguistic activity to an abstract verbal pattern in this way. But the reification is irresistibly convenient, and harmless enough if its limitations are constantly borne in mind. Figure 4.1 shows what is involved. The lines inside and around the

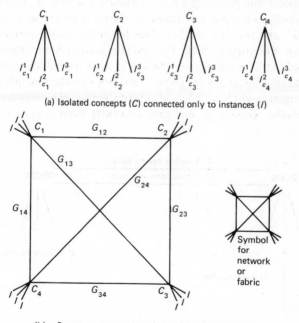

(a) Isolated concepts (C) connected only to instances (I)

(b) Concepts now connected to each other by verbal generalisations (G) as well as to instances

FIGURE 4.1 *Conceptual fabrics*

square stand for generalisations, and those radiating outwards connect concepts to instances. The whole figure represents the basic
form of any conceptual fabric. (Cf. Hesse, 1974, 1980. Hesse's 'network model' is very close to what is here called the 'conceptual
fabric'.)

What are the implications of the existence of conceptual fabrics
of this kind? One is that some everyday notions of the process of
learning have to be revised. We tend to think of distinct acts of
learning, each one related to a distinct concept: this verbal definition or act of ostension teaches us about this specific concept; the
next teaches us about another; and so on. But such an atomistic conception is inadequate. Let us go back to learning about ducks and
geese again (cf. Chapter 2), but this time let us introduce explicit
verbal generalisations between the two terms (cf. Figure 4.2, which
should, of course, be visualised as a part of a much larger conceptual
fabric, into which many more generalisations run from both 'duck'
and 'goose'). Imagine that a new candidate instance, X, is encountered which, as before, resembles yet differs from earlier instances
of 'duck', and that the teacher gives his authoritative pronouncement that X is indeed a duck. This time the learner is simultaneously
informed that X is not a goose. Now X in itself resembles yet differs
from existing instances of 'goose', and prior to the teacher's pronouncement might have been adjudged a goose. *Hence, in learning
about ducks, knowledge has simultaneously been acquired about*

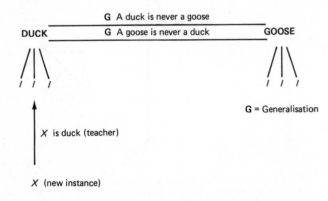

FIGURE 4.2   *Learning and the conceptual fabric*

[Handwritten marginal note: against atomism in concept learning. In learning more about ducks and also learn more about geese.]

geese. *X* represents an area in perceptual space into which usage of the concept 'goose' should not be extended. Thus we see that the proper usage of concepts can be learned, indeed must be learned, from the outside, as it were, as well as from within. We learn where the usage of a particular concept should not be extended by learning instances of other concepts which are recognised as necessarily alternative to that concept. There is no other way of learning this information about the confines within which similarity relations should develop.

This means that there is no way of acquiring knowledge in a genuinely step-by-step manner, with each step being completely understood and justified before moving on to the next. The knowledge associated with any part of a conceptual fabric is only fully acquired when the whole fabric has been acquired. Conceptual fabrics, including those in the natural sciences, have the character of hermeneutic systems; all that has been written of such systems and how they must be understood applies in the context of science.

conceptual fabrics as hermeneutic systems.

Parallel conclusions can be drawn concerning the use and the evaluation of knowledge. As well as being learned as a whole, knowledge is related to experience as a whole. To use a concept is to appraise an instance in terms of an entire fabric. To evaluate a generalisation is to evaluate the over-all pattern of generalisations within the fabric. No statement or concept can be isolated so that its truth or appropriateness can be studied in isolation. This was pointed out long ago by Duhem, who took a number of particular scientific hypotheses and demonstrated how in every case their standing in relation to observation, or the results of experiment, could not be evaluated without reference to whole sets of connected hypotheses. He concluded that 'To seek to separate each of the hypotheses of theoretical physics from the other assumptions on which this science rests in order to subject it in isolation to observational test is to pursue a chimera; for the realisation and interpretation of no matter what experiment in physics imply adherence to a whole set of theoretical propositions' (Duhem, 1954, pp. 199–200). From time to time optimistic philosophers have attempted to discover exceptions to this claim, or even general arguments which would suffice to refute it altogether, but the consequence of this has merely been to establish Duhem's assertion as one of the best-grounded findings ever to emerge from the philosophy of science.

Unfortunately, Duhem's actual examples are inconveniently technical, and I shall use a very simple hypothetical instance for purposes of illustration here. Consider the conceptual fabric in Figure 4.3, and imagine that the hypothesis 'species breed true' is to be tested. To this end, a putative species 'goose' is chosen, and members of this species collected, and induced to breed. Imagine that some of the resulting offspring are of a form which we are not disposed to allow as geese: that is, imagine that the breeding experiment throws up a *prima facie* disconfirmation of our hypothesis. Duhem's point here is that the results of the experiment can always be blamed on the inadequacy of a *different* hypothesis in the relevant system. In Figure 4.3, for example, the other generalisation — that geese constitute a species — could be held to be the source of inadequacy, *not* the hypothesis concerning the behaviour of species.

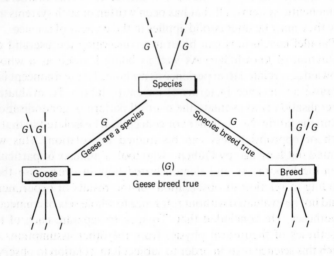

FIGURE 4.3   *Evaluation and the conceptual fabric*

Consider now the possibility of outflanking Duhem by moving to the hypothesis 'geese breed true': is not this, in isolation, disconfirmed by the above experiment? Not so, because just as geese can be said not to be a species in the first case, so particular 'geese' used in the experiment can be said not to be genuine geese after all. Certainly, to reject the status of the birds used as geese might count against other generalisations involving the term 'geese' — say, 'only geese, among birds, eat grass'. But this is merely to reiterate Duhem's point. The 'geese breed true' hypothesis can be saved by shifting the problems raised by experiment over to other hypotheses in the conceptual fabric.

In the last analysis Duhem's position is simply a variant of the finitist account of concept application discussed in section 2.3 above. A hypothesis can never be conclusively tested because of our discretion in the application of concepts: it is up to us whether we continue to take 'goose' as a species, or continue to take particular instances as genuine instances of 'goose'. The way we apply terms, and the extent to which we accept generalisations, are no more than different sides of the same coin. A decision as to how to attach a concept to nature is at the same time a decision as to how it should connect to other concepts. A concept–concept link can be maintained by applying the concepts to instances appropriately, and, conversely, a concept–instance link can be maintained by appropriate linkage of that concept and other concepts.

The flexibility and the revisability of the processes whereby we attach instances to terms guarantees that Duhem's assertion will always apply. Indeed, it does more than this. Not only, as a result, is reality incapable of giving the lie to an isolated hypothesis; it is no more capable of indicating the existence of deficiency in a whole set of connected hypotheses. A whole conceptual fabric can always be *made out* as in perfect accord with experience, if the community sustaining it is of a mind to do so. There are a number of ways of making this point clear and evident. Perhaps the quickest is to note that no over-all system of verbal culture is of its very nature closed and completed. New concepts and new generalisations can always be added to the conceptual fabric. Hence, whenever anything of nuisance value arises out of experience, it can always be deemed a new kind of thing or event, and assimilated under a new concept, leaving the existing structure unaltered. Members of a culture may always have it, if they wish, that their generalisations apply only to those phenomena which confirm them: there need be no anomalies in such a culture, only phenomena awaiting names. Such a culture can be used by members as an instrument, employed where it is useful, not employed where it is not.

It is tempting to conclude that the conceptual fabrics of the natural sciences have the character of unfalsifiable systems, but, strictly speaking, this is not quite correct. Unfalsifiability is not an intrinsic property of a fabric. We should say merely that scientists, if they so desire, can always maintain their verbal culture as an unfalsifiable system. This conclusion, however, is quite sufficient to confirm Kuhn's analysis in the preceding section: all the intractable formal problems of evaluation which he identifies follow readily once it is accepted.

Any actual conceptual fabric is, of course, more than a collection of empirically exemplified terms, crudely associated together. The generalisations which link terms to each other can vary enormously in their form. Instead of 'birds fly', it may be held that they usually do, or probably do, or always do, or by definition do, or in reality do, or of their nature do. Although their use does not invalidate anything so far argued, it is worth giving very brief consideration to the many qualifying terms which impute probability, degree of belief, moral certainty, analyticity, necessity, ontological significance, and so on, to the various connecting threads of the conceptual fabric.

To those employing such terms, their use is simply part of the complex task of representing, within the system of knowledge, the character of experience. But since experience does not force the use of these terms, it is open to us to examine their incidence from a sociological perspective, concentrating upon the people applying the terms more than upon that to which they are applied. We can ask, without implying any criticism, why people employ these terms, what ends they are put to, what tasks they perform. What communal strategies are reflected in the use of one type of generalisation rather than another (cf. also section 5.2 to follow)?

Terms indicating frequency or reliability have a clear practical utility. By qualifying generalisations with 'sometimes', 'often', 'probably', and so on, we can adjust the conceptual fabric as a technical, predictive instrument. Such qualifications are open to continuing revision as we interact with our environment. We possess inherent associative and inductive proclivities which dispose us to place increased reliance on generalisations which are confirmed in the course of routine unreflective concept application along lines established by socialisation. And conversely, we tend to weaken, qualify or circumvent those generalisations which lead to dashed expectations in the course of our routine practice. The result can be a tendency over time for the distribution of terms indicating frequency and reliability to move to whatever confers a maximum of instrumental advantage in relation to a given pattern of social activity and social objectives.

But what of the other terms, which impute certainty, analyticity, necessity, ontological significance and the like to many of the generalisations in a conceptual fabric? The use of these terms can also be understood as a matter of communal strategy. Consider, for example, the claim that a generalisation stands as a matter of definition, as a tautology, or, as philosophers sometimes say to much the same effect, as an analytic statement. To accept such a claim is to agree to isolate the generalisation from experience. 'Birds fly' is a generalisation we can feel free to modify: if something turns up which seems to us a bird, yet which is flightless, we can simply say that it has transpired after all that only most birds fly. But on the other hand, were we to accept that birds, as a matter of definition, fly, then no empirical phenomenon would in itself dispose us to revise our view: any problematic flightless phenomenon would be, whatever else, not a bird. The problem of assimilating such a phenomenon would have to be solved at some other point in the conceptual fabric; the relation between birds and flight would remain unchanged.

In agreeing upon what is analytic and what is not, a community agrees upon a strategy of concept application and cultural change. Analytic generalisations are to be left in place; other generalisations are more immediately revisable (see Figure 4.4). The day-to-day

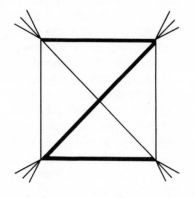

Conceptual fabric with fixed sub-structure (▬) of
analytic relations within over-all structure of
empirical generalisations (—), cf. Figure 4.1

FIGURE 4.4   *Analytic relationships*

adjustments of the conceptual fabric inspired by immediate practical empirical problems fall upon the non-analytic generalisations and the arrangements of instances under concepts.

Such a two-tier system of generalisations can have great practical convenience; it can, for example, facilitate communication through a culture. By endowing some generalisations with long-term stability and protecting them from much of the effect of day-to-day adjustment, they are made available for use as the taken-for-granted backdrop essential to all discourse. They serve as important shared understandings which will be present when interaction is attempted even between widely separated members of a highly dynamic culture. If all generalisations were equally available for minor modification and adjustment, background understandings would be more difficult to find or to create, and the on-going problems of communication and intelligibility in a culture would be exacerbated. As to which parts of a fabric are stabilised, that is a matter of communal agreement, and wholly contingent.

This kind of analysis, it must be emphasised, does not imply the existence of two kinds of generalisation with different intrinsic properties. What is actually being spoken of is two extreme kinds of *policy* which people may adopt towards their generalisations. The analytic propositions of a community are, as it were, those which the community is trying hardest to hold stable at a particular time. Analytic propositions are intrinsically no more immune to experience or exempt from adjustment than any others; they are merely those which a particular community, *as a matter of convention*, is currently treating as analytic. As the practice of a community alters, so too does the status of its generalisations. Yesterday's empirical claims may be made today's analytic truths; or the analytic statements of days gone by may be demoted into mere empirical generalisations — and false ones at that (cf. Quine, 1953).

In the history and philosophy of science it is well known that scientific laws may oscillate between the empirical and the analytic in this way. Newton's laws of motion serve as standard examples. Kuhn's discussion of Dalton's law of constant composition points to another instance. But although these examples are so familiar, and well-recognised work like that of Quine is available to indicate their significance, analyticity is still not perceived as a sociologically interesting phenomenon. Analyticity continues to be treated as an intrinsic property of statements rather than as the product of a continuing communally implemented policy.

Let us move on now to a second and final example. Consider the language of Platonism, of appearances and reality, of the shadows on the cave wall and the underlying essence of things. This mode of discourse can be employed to much the same end as the language of synonymy and analyticity: it can serve to stabilise part of a conceptual fabric. In this case, however, the protection of one generalisation does not require change anywhere else in the system, or the invention of new kinds of thing. The language of Platonism is capable of being used to maintain any form of verbal culture as a set of necessary truths in perfect correspondence with any experience at all. Not surprisingly, such an extremely powerful linguistic resource is found invaluable in all cultures.

Suppose that we draw a very large number of triangles and in each case measure the sum of their angles; and suppose that our average result is 179.90 degrees ± 0.01. It is unlikely that we should allow this result to disturb our conviction that the angles of a triangle add up to 180 degrees. What might be said is that our drawings are imperfect manifestations of what a triangle really is. In essence, a triangle is an ideal form which just does have angles adding up to 180 degrees; it is to this ideal form that the term 'triangle' properly refers — all real triangles are essentially identical in having their angles exactly equal to 180 degrees. Along similar lines, it might be said that the term 'electron' denotes an essence, and properly applies only to particles which are identical in essence, i.e. in the essential properties of mass and charge. Actual measured instances will doubtless reveal, on superficial interpretation, variations of mass and charge from particle to particle; but these measurements are just the shadows on the cave wall, giving a clue to the true reality, wherein mass and charge are in all cases identical. The variations in the measurements are either the result of error, or due to the presence of unknown additional entities associated with the electrons being measured. One can even be a realist about ducks and geese; indeed, perhaps one should be. The generalisation 'ducks fly' survives endless counter-examples — baby ducks, injured ducks, exhausted ducks, indolent ducks, and so on. It could be said by way of justification that the term refers to an essence, an ideal of duck manifested to various degrees in actual instances; whatever these instances actually do, the generalisation 'ducks fly' remains true of the essential nature of ducks.

Just as in the previous case, these strategies stabilise a conceptual fabric only to the extent that communities of language users turn them to that end. What are taken as the underlying essences in nature is a matter of convention, and subject to variation from time to time. The essences of yesteryear may be dismissed today as non-existent or as metaphysical garbage; or they may be retained as convenient fictions, or as mere clusters of particulars — in science, think of phlogiston, light rays, latent heat, Radiata (cf. Winsor, 1976), acids, bases and salts. The essences of today are vulnerable to similar fates in the future, as communal practice changes; there is no way of protecting them from change by asserting that they, unlike earlier essences, are really present in nature. Such assertions are merely part of the activity of sustaining our present conventions, and will themselves change as these conventions change.

In sociology the use of the language of essences to stabilise conceptual fabrics is understood as *reification*. A reified cosmos, wherein fluctuating processes are made out as manifestations of underlying unchanging essences, is seen as a reactionary ideological device which sets apparently objective limits on the possibilities for change, and dampens human aspirations. Belief in an underlying essential human nature is often cited as an example of reification.

This, however, is a far too narrow approach to such a valuable and versatile tool as the language of essentialism. We should first examine how the tool works, and then ask what it might profitably be used to do.

The language of essences disconnects concepts from a direct relationship with their instances (see Figure 4.5). Instances become mere appearances, shadows on the cave wall, providing no more than clues to the essences which are the actual referents of concepts. A story can be inserted to make an instance relate to a concept in whatever manner is required. Every appearance can be made out as essence + overlying contingencies + errors of perception. This does indeed offer a superb defensive resource, which, like the appeal to analyticity, can be used to protect generalisations (cf. section 3.4 above). But it can also be used in quite the opposite way: to decouple a conceptual fabric from instances may facilitate the task of changing it. To treat instances as unreliable appearances legitimates re-orderings of the connections within the fabric of concepts and generalisations. The fabric is made out as a provisional attempt to match the relationship between essences which appertains in

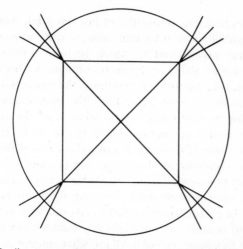

Realist strategy decoupling or allowing play between
instances and concepts (cf. Figure 4.1)

FIGURE 4.5   *Realism*

reality; concepts are made out as imperfectly defined and instantiated at the present time and in need of continuing transformation towards the ideal system; instances are conceived as fallible allocations of imperfectly known things to imperfectly defined terms.

Essentialism employed in this way can both legitimate and organise the introduction of major innovations in the natural sciences. It was noted in section 4.1 how Dalton's atomic theory at the time it was first introduced appeared to be incompatible with most of the existing observations and experimental results in chemistry. To those willing to think, explicitly or implicitly, along essentialist lines, this would have been a far less formidable objection than it might at first appear. Existing results could have been made out as appearances, and the changes in the conceptual fabric required by Dalton could have been treated as a move towards the representation of the underlying reality. Instances and experimental results could then have been re-assimilated to the new structure by re-interpretation, re-allocation of error, and in some cases repetition of the experiments themselves. (This hypothetical account is in fact probably a tolerable thumbnail-sketch of what actually happened.)

No great proportion of natural scientists explicitly advocates essentialism. None the less the form of their discourse is almost invariably, even if only implicitly, of just this kind. And given the range of possibilities both for imposing pattern and adapting pattern, simultaneously if need be, which the form of the language of essences makes available to the using community, this is not to be wondered at. Like any other community, the community of scientists is responsible both for the authoritative maintenance of knowledge and for its continuing development, and the two can run together beautifully as communal activities in the framework provided by an essentialist idiom. It can indeed reasonably be asked whether the essentialist mode of cognition (as opposed to any particular theory of essences) is not simply the general mode of cognition of any human community, deriving from innate structures involved in the epigenesis of linguistic and inferential skills. All cultures have to organise an unimaginably complex environment by use of a few thousand symbols. All use what amount to essentialist strategies in doing so, and use them both securely and creatively. Nor is it easy to imagine what alternative modes of discourse could replace them.

Current perceptions of essentialism and the realist mode of speaking are unduly restricted, both in the social sciences and in philosophy. In the former, although essentialism is recognised as a strategy, its possibilities are not fully recognised. Reifying metaphysics are charged with stultifying thought, concealing processes as things, and consequently encouraging resignation and political passivity. But this is to take account only of a single mode of use of a realist mode of speech. And worse, it is to impute to ideas what should properly be imputed to their users.

Conversely, in philosophy there is awareness of the value and ubiquitousness of essentialism, but it is not analysed as a strategy. Instead, philosophers argue that since the realist mode of speech is so widespread and effective, particularly in the natural sciences, physical nature must surely be constituted of essences underlying the appearances of phenomena (cf. Putnam, 1975). This argument from how we speak to the ultimate nature of reality would be implausible in the best of circumstances, but given our present knowledge of the history of science, and the fate of such essences as phlogiston, caloric and ether, it is singularly lacking in force.

Putative essences and their varied fates can only be understood by accepting that verbal culture is a resource of the community sustaining it. Essences are among the means we employ to tune the instrument which is our verbal culture so that it organises and assimilates information with what for us is maximum effectiveness. From this instrumentalist viewpoint, what some actual community treats as real is not a problem for philosophy or for physical science: it is a sociological problem involving examination of what the community sets as the tasks of its culture, and how specific realist strategies can prove conducive to those tasks. This, of course, is not to make the positive claim that no real essences exist underlying natural phenomena: to assert that, as much as to assert its opposite, would be to indulge in a form of ontological speculation which sociological research could never hope to justify.

4.3 Evaluation and normal science

Kuhn's account of normal science is a fascinating and insightful description of a conventional activity. Yet he himself occasionally encourages us to forget this. His discussion of the insufficiency of logic and experience at a time of paradigm change can create the impression that at other times they *are* sufficient. He even occasionally refers to normal research as 'cumulative', which as a common-sense description is reasonable enough, but which evokes all the wrong associations for those philosophers who deeply desire to make out as much as possible of the history of science as 'rational progress'. Thus encouraged, some of these have argued that the meaning of concepts is stable and unproblematic in periods of normal science, so that 'rational evaluation' is possible therein: only the discontinuities in meaning at times of revolution create problems for orthodox philosophical accounts of scientific judgement. (Cf. my own suggestion in section 4.1 that it is only at these points of discontinuity, where one mode of conventional activity is replaced by another, that problems could possibly arise for a sociological understanding of scientific judgement.)

Scheffler (1967) is a philosopher who finds the discussion of incommensurable paradigms the disturbing feature in Kuhn's work. He seeks to eliminate the 'problem' of incommensurability by establishing a relationship between the meanings of terms before and after revolutions: in particular, he looks for overlaps of reference or extension, wrongly assuming that revolutions change the sense of terms but not what they refer to in nature. Martin (1971) recognises that sense and reference, intension and extension, are both changed by revolutions, but he also seeks for equivalences in meanings, with the same aim as Scheffler. Both men treat revolutions as problematic episodes in an otherwise straightforward historical development. Normal science is assumed to involve evaluations which conform to traditional philosophical accounts. The 'threat' Kuhn poses to the 'objectivity' of science can be eliminated simply by finding a method of applying extensional semantics and 'logical' methods of comparison to statements drawn from opposite sides of a revolutionary divide.

Scheffler and Martin have laboured under a massive if excusable misapprehension. Kuhn's work does not indicate occasional points where their notion of 'objectivity' is inapplicable; it demonstrates the total irrelevance of the notion. All the problems of evaluation which disturb philosophers because they imply the presence of a 'social' dimension and thus the insufficiency of autonomous 'reason' are found throughout normal science. The maintenance and development of routine usage is every bit as much a social phenomenon as the radically innovative changes of usage which Kuhn cites in his account of revolutions. The substance of Kuhn's account of normal science is finitist (cf. section 2.3, which is a much more potent refutation of the approach of Scheffler and Martin than the present brief discussion). Normal scientists are not rational automata, using words according to their inherent meanings or extensions. Existing usage always leaves future usage to be developed by users themselves. It is precisely because of this that the *continuing* role of authority and social control is of ineradicable significance in normal science. Normal scientists cannot be impressed with the similarity relations of a scientific specialty by authority, and then left to themselves as individuals, to be looked after, as it were, by the implications of those similarity relations. A similarity relation cannot function as an instruction which tells a rational automaton how to behave; on the contrary, it is a resource which must be sustained and developed by collective human agency. This is the profound sense in which normal science is a social activity. And this is why Kuhn's matter-of-fact account of routine scientific activity threatens epistemological orthodoxy more radically even than his explicitly philosophical discussion of revolutionary states of affairs.

Consider an example identified as normal science by Kuhn himself, and already briefly mentioned in the previous chapter. In section 3.2 the problem-solution of the point-mass pendulum was described, as was the way it was extended to compute the speed of a swinging or rolling solid mass at the bottom of its descent. Later, Bernoulli's calculation of the speed of efflux of a liquid from an orifice in a vessel became a further accepted achievement of normal science, by extension of these earlier problem-solutions. This evaluation of Bernoulli's work, however, depended upon it being accepted that liquids could manifest speed in 'the same' way as solids. However this acceptance developed, whether from familiar cases of the speeds of solids to problems involving liquids, or vice versa, it involved no scientific revolution. Yet such a development cannot at all be understood as predetermined by the very meaning of the term 'speed', or as a deductive inference from a definition of 'speed'. Assuming that consideration of liquids was historically the later, conceptions of speed in respect of liquids must have been a development by analogy with understood instances and conceptions of speed in the realm of solids. And at the point when instances of the speed of liquids were first used to teach the term 'speed', that term became systematically linked to nature in a recognisably new way; its 'meaning' was transformed.

Note that in this case, when the 'speed' of liquids was first talked of, it would have been open to the community involved to reject the implied analogy, to insist that it involved incorrect usage, and to maintain that 'speed' was a term with reference only to solids. Alternatively, what in a liquid was to count as 'the same' as the speed of a solid could have been decided differently. It is a contingent sequence of such developments of usage which has constructed the current concept of 'speed', which applies in far from self-evident ways to the motion of rigid objects, of liquids, of waves 'travelling' through liquids, of springs vibrating back and forth, of wheels, and so on. 'Speed' is a similarity relation, an agreed cluster of non-identical instances or applications (cf. section 2.4); and the applications are built up in an unpredictable historical development involving continuing modification of meaning.

Meaning change does not occur simply at times of revolution. It occurs all the time, producing formal problems of evaluation all the time. If there are such episodes as scientific revolutions, they are not periods when a special kind of cultural change occurs which

[margin note: meaning change as an ongoing process]

generates unusual formal problems of evaluation. Any particular change which occurs in a revolutionary episode can occur equally in a period of normal science, whether it be meaning change, technical change, the invention of new problem-solutions, or the emergence of new standards of judgement. If there is anything worth calling a revolutionary episode, it is a period when a large number of cultural changes all occur at once, or when scientists find themselves obliged to opt for one or other alternative cluster of practices and beliefs. The concept of scientific revolution is suited to historical narrative. For the narrow sociological end of identifying basic processes of cultural change it is irrelevant.

Once more we are led to the conclusion that Kuhn's insistence upon the 'necessity' of scientific revolutions is misplaced (cf. Kuhn, 1970, ch. 9). There is nothing in normal science to prohibit any particular kind of development, in technique, in problem-solutions or in verbal culture. Hence there is nothing to compel a leap out of the system: nothing makes it necessary to replace, rather than to develop, existing practice. Perhaps Kuhn's own conviction of the necessity of revolutions arises from an incorrect appraisal of what is possible under the rubric of normal science. It is worth pointing out that major cultural change can be brought about not just by the accumulation of many small deviations from routine, or extensions of routine, over a period of time, but even by activity carried out in meticulous conformity to routine.

Imagine that two colours are taken, say green and yellow. Next, a hundred intermediate shades are produced, running in a series from the former to the latter. If any two adjacent colours in the series are perceptibly different, then a hundred intermediate shades are constructed between them. This strategy is continued until no colour is perceptibly different from its immediate neighbour in the series. Routine application of the term 'green' can now begin at one end of the series and end at the other, with 'green' referring to yellow. Stretch the series of applications over a long period and assume that earlier applications are forgotten and drop away from the similarity relation 'green', which is constituted only of recently pointed-out instances. Now routine usage can move from one point on the spectrum to another without anyone being aware of any meaning change — indeed, in a sense, without any such change having occurred. A sense that there has been cultural change can now only be generated by a historical investigation which resurrects both earlier usage and the entities referred to in the course of it. Such an investigation, leaping back over many years of routine usage, would thereby almost certainly produce such a strong sense of contrast in linguistic practice that routine would be said to have undergone a massive change.

To look at widely separated points in a span of normal science can likewise produce the conviction that massive cultural changes and shifts of meaning have occurred. Historians occasionally remark that the tenets of modern chemical atomism are almost exactly the opposite of Dalton's originals, and that the associated practice has also changed profoundly. The plentiful examples of this kind suggest that there are no limits to the flexibility and adaptability of research traditions. (Cf. also the historical material in Edge and Mulkay, 1976.)

The problem of meaning variance occurs everywhere in science, as in culture generally. It is no less a problem where usage is routine and unthinking than where it is self-consciously developed and extended. Accordingly, everything in science, every act of concept application, every inference, every judgement, is of sociological interest. In normal science even the most routine steps are interesting, not simply as symbols of conformity to authoritatively prescribed procedures or assumptions, but as displays of what such conformity consists in, and even as contributions to establishing what such conformity should consist in. The presentation of routine findings, as routine findings, helps to sustain the general sense of what is routine: as much as an act of social conformity, it is a form of social control.

Processes of evaluation in science, whether in 'normal' or 'revolutionary' periods, are not sufficiently determined by logic and experiment alone. Nor are they intelligible as logical implications of conventions or communally accepted standards. Both these views fail to make intelligible the *judgements of sameness* which scientists make in deciding what the facts actually are. There are now a number of empirical sociological studies which expose this failure and reveal judgements of sameness as contingent, on-the-spot decisions. Among them are Collins (1975 and 1981), Wynne (1976), Latour and Woolgar (1979), Shapin (1979), not to mention their precursor, but in every way their peer, Ludwik Fleck in his *Genesis and Development of a Scientific Fact* (first published in 1935).

Collins's study of gravity-wave detection (1975), although the first of the recent studies of evaluation, remains among the more interesting. It is based upon interviews with scientists who, following reports of the detection of gravitational waves in 1969, attempted to replicate the initial experiment, and to that end themselves constructed devices designed to detect gravity waves. The knowledge claim being checked by these scientists was a highly controversial one, deliberately selected by Collins to allow facts to be looked at 'while they are being formed, before they have become "set" as part of anyone's natural (scientific) world' (1975, pp. 205–6). None the less it was agreed that gravitational radiation was a reputable physical phenomenon (predicted by general relativity theory), that astronomical events such as star collapses should produce large amounts of the radiation, and that the building of a gravity-wave detector was a possibility given the currently available research techniques. Nor was the particular detector employed in the initial research thought to be seriously misconceived. What was generally regarded as suspect about the initial results was the sheer strength of the signals recorded, which appeared at levels difficult to reconcile theoretically with any plausible real source and mechanism of production.

Those who undertook to replicate this initial work proceeded to build their own apparatus for gravity-wave detection. Such apparatus was not, however, conceived as an indistinguishable replica of the original. Any particular apparatus was considered by its designers to be 'the same' as the original, to the extent that both were describable as 'gravity-wave detectors'; but it was also considered to be different, typically 'better' in important respects. It might be a 'better' receiver, or have 'better' electronics, or a 'better' computer program for processing inputs, or 'better' statistics. These judgements of quality were legitimated by reference to standard scientific beliefs about nature, technique, procedure, etc., such as are used routinely in the course of normal science. But Collins reveals strong divergences in these very judgements, both with regard to the extent of sameness, and to the qualitative rankings of the merits of the various replications. There was no consensus concerning which were the best detectors, which the most closely related detectors, or even whether all the alternative designs deserved to be regarded as 'detectors': what was to *count* as a detector was controversial, despite it being perceived as something which could be worked out from current physics. Finally, and not surprisingly given the above, there was evident disagreement concerning the value of the results obtained from the various 'replications'.

There are a number of intriguing hints in Collins's paper as to why these disagreements existed. For example, it is suggested that usage of the term 'replication' was related to the perceived structure of recognition and reward. The original experimenter claimed to have repeated his own results consistently, and to have improved his own methods over time in a number of ways. But his sequence of work was not treated by other scientists as a sequence of independent replications of the initial finding, even though it could have been argued that the experiments in his sequence were more obviously 'the same' than any others. The very idea of replication seemed to involve the notion of *recognised variation* from the initial work. And in producing such variation scientists looked to their own repertoires of competence and expertise, 'improving' that part of the experiment most susceptible to their own peculiar skills (cf. Collins, 1975, pp. 210–11). Scientists noted that 'carbon-copy' repetition would either produce different results to the original, when there would be nothing to say which were the better, or similar results, which would merely secure recognition for the initial experimenter. Replication with an 'improved' detector would be more rewarding. Different results could be claimed to override the original ones, because of the more advanced design of the detector. Similar results could be held properly to establish what had previously been doubtful, again because of the improvement in design. Hence it was expedient for scientists to stress the differences between their own work and the initial experiment, and to see the replications of others as too much the same as that initial work.

This general approach to understanding the various judgements of similarity and difference in the case study is very plausible (cf. section 5.2). Unfortunately, Collins is unable, indeed he does not attempt, to develop and establish it in detail. His main objective, in which he succeeds admirably, is to show that what counts as a replication, as the same as what has gone before, is neither determined by logic and experience nor inferable from accepted physical knowledge or scientific standards. By displaying the conflicting judgements of highly competent scientists, judgements which simply do not invite explanation by reference to error, bias or superficiality, Collins shows how misleading it is to talk of the 'implications' of

[margin note: interesting: what counts as a replication]

existing knowledge. Different scientists inferred different, conflicting things from existing knowledge. Existing physical knowledge was incapable of telling scientists what was a gravity-wave detector and what was not. The scientists had to develop usage themselves. Collectively they had to seek to agree upon what should be called a 'gravity-wave detector', and hence what it should mean to say that a gravity-wave detection experiment was a competent one. When Collins wrote such an agreement had not been achieved. If and when it is, 'gravity wave' will become the similarity relation that clusters all the processed readings of the recognised 'competent' experiments together as one thing. (Cf. Collins, 1981, for an account of more recent developments, which include the achievement of a consensus concerning the status of the initial experimental results.)

4.4   The boundaries of science

There is a further task of evaluation which scientists find themselves required to perform, but which so far has not been considered at all. As well as evaluating the research of themselves and their peers, they have to define who those peers are. In conjunction with the rest of society, they must decide what is a scientific field and what is a pseudo-scientific one, what is a properly scientific argument and what is not, what science can pronounce upon and what it cannot. And such decisions relate to issues of great moment, concerning which expert is to be believed, which institutions are given credibility, where cognitive authority is to lie, and ultimately what kind of society we are to live in.

If evaluation within science necessarily takes place by the active interpretation of conventions, then so too must the evaluation of what counts as science. The boundary between the scientific and the non-scientific must itself be a convention, generated by social processes. Hence to understand where this boundary actually falls requires, not the formulation of any principle of demarcation, but rather the empirical study of those social processes whereby the boundary is made visible and sustained.

There is now a considerable amount of research material which focuses upon boundary maintenance around the sub-culture of science (cf. Wallace, 1979; Collins and Pinch, forthcoming). The processes involved are no different from those generally found when sub-cultures are demarcated. None the less, because of the importance of this particular boundary it can be startling and salutary to be shown how it is actually kept in place. Appropriate material is provided in a recent study of parapsychology by Collins and Pinch (1979).

Paranormal phenomena are those which are physically impossible according to generally accepted scientific opinion. Parapsychological phenomena, accordingly, are those which require to be explained in terms of extra-sensory perception (ESP) and analogous notions. An important class of such phenomena is generated by requiring subjects to guess the outcome of events of which they can have no knowledge. Evidence has been presented that a few individuals can guess successfully in such situations to a degree which is inconsistent with hypotheses of chance variation. Parapsychology is the field concerned with such phenomena and their nature: to be a parapsychologist is at least to take seriously the possibility that such phenomena exist.

Collins and Pinch note how some parapsychologists sought to have their field recognised as a legitimate scientific discipline. To this end, they operated as far as possible like orthodox occupants of a scientific role, and they sought publication of their work in accepted scientific journals. This in turn required that their legitimacy be recognised by those in respectable, fully accepted scientific fields, something which proved not at all easy to achieve. The scepticism of a significant number of orthodox scientists led to a controversy over the scientific status of parapsychology.

The main legitimating move made by the parapsychologists themselves was to point to what they considered as their impeccable methodological credentials. The phenomena they addressed were problematic, but their work embodied all the features of 'scientific method'. Appropriate statistical techniques were used; advanced electronics generated random numbers for use in experiments; 'double blind' and analogous methods for eliminating experimenter interference were employed: 'It seems likely that the best of modern parapsychology comprises some of the most rigorously controlled and methodologically sophisticated work in the sciences' (Collins and Pinch, 1979, pp. 243–4).

Despite this, however, many orthodox scientists were still disposed to deny parapsychology the status of a legitimate scientific activity. An extensive list of their grounds for such a denial is pro-

[handwritten margin note: nice — the rejection of ESP]

vided by Collins and Pinch. They fall into two classes: there are grounds which are never invoked in the evaluation of accepted disciplines; and grounds which employ the knowledge of accepted disciplines as reference criteria. In the first class are claims that parapsychology is trivial, uninteresting and weakly developed theoretically. Scientists have also felt free, in its case, to cite 'prejudice' as the cause of their reservations, and to point to the possibility that all the problematic results in the field are the consequence of fraud. In the second class is the claim that, on pain of violating 'Occam's razor', all possible existing natural mechanisms must be conclusively eliminated before ESP is postulated. Then there are the simpler claims that ESP contradicts existing science and hence 'logic', or analogously that ESP is not part of existing science, and hence not part of 'experience'.

Here, then, is an account of the negotiations through which the boundaries of science were actually laid down over a particular sector of our cultural terrain. And not just the insufficiency, but the sheer carelessness of the arguments, particularly from the establishment side, is very striking. If orthodoxy were not disposed to accept the parapsychologists' claims, it might surely have produced more refined legitimations for rejecting them. The legitimations actually used are all too obvious special pleading. The standards they invoke appear as special devices taken up for a specific task of demolition; it is impossible to credit their status as universal, consistently employed grounds for scientific judgement. Were the formal properties of legitimations of any real importance, these would surely do disservice to their own cause.

It is valuable to be made aware in this way of how thin is the rhetoric, and how superficial the discourse, which accompanies the placing of such an important boundary as that between science and pseudo-science. Nor should the example be regarded as atypical. Quite the contrary is likely to prove the case, at least in so far as the scientific establishment is involved in the boundary-drawing process. Practising natural scientists are on the whole neither accomplished casuists, nor people to set great store by verbal rationalisations; their shortcomings in these respects have been documented before (Grazia, 1966).

The example also serves, however, to reveal how trivial are these shortcomings. After crash courses in logic and rhetoric, our established experts might well display an increased competence in the art of legitimation, and hide more effectively the contingent basis of their judgements. But they would not be able to change the basic character of the judgements themselves, or of the legitimations invoked to buttress them. To assess the scientific status of parapsychology, with its 'methodological innocence and theoretical guilt' (Allison, 1979, p. 288), would still require more than 'reason'; and any legitimations such an assessment evoked would consequently be of the kind already considered (cf. also the extended discussion in Collins and Pinch, forthcoming).

From a sociological point of view there is little more to be said about this example, or about the boundary of science in general. The boundary is a convention: it surrounds a finite cluster of concrete instances of science without implying that there is any essence which they share; the instances are the accumulated outcome of a historical process of negotiation. Any attempt to eject instances from the cluster, or to add instances presently rejected, is to employ the term 'science' in an evaluative sense, and to participate in the process of boundary-drawing which, as sociological observers, we should be describing.

Epistemologists sometimes say that to reject any stipulative definition of science is to be without recourse against the various collections of incompetents who occasionally decide to constitute themselves as a science. All such incompetents have to do, it is said, is to conform to whatever collection of imbecile routines they choose, call themselves 'Xologists', and publish papers which cite each other lavishly and stress how terribly scientific they all are; at this point it must be acknowledged, in the absence of a stipulative definition, that 'Xology' is a science or a scientific specialty.

In practice, however, communities do evaluate one 'ology' without reference to any other, and often they refuse any standing to the 'ology' in question. Nor would recourse to epistemologists assist such evaluation, since epistemology is not an emanation of 'reason' but is made up of doctrines and standards which themselves demand evaluation. One does not gain exemption from evaluation by claiming to be rational, any more than by claiming to be scientific. In the last analysis a community evaluates all its cognitive authorities in relation to its over-all way of life, not by reference to a specific set of verbal standards. No doubt this is how the scientific establishment actually evaluates parapsychology. And should sociologists ever seek to separate proper competence from institutionalised idiocy, in their own field or elsewhere, the same basis for judgement is available to them.

5

Developments

5.1 Ethnomethodology

In this final chapter I examine some recent developments in the sociology of scientific knowledge, and end by relating its problems and findings to general issues in the development of sociological theory. Several earlier themes will reappear as I proceed, so that as well as pointing forward the discussion will serve also to some extent as a recapitulation. Note, however, that what follows is neither a survey of current research nor an attempt to assess the importance of Kuhn's work in that research. I merely seek to outline some interesting themes and ideas and explore how they might be fitted together.

First, since science is a typical form of culture, ethnomethodological methods should apply to it as well, or as badly, as they apply elsewhere. I am not a card-carrying ethnomethodologist, and cannot claim to be qualified to dispense its mysteries. I am aware also of the great variation of views within the field, and the impossibility of describing it to the satisfaction of all its practitioners. None the less, since ethnomethodology constitutes one of the most important of all developments in (or for) sociological theory, I have risked a brief account of some of its themes, and their significance in the present context. I shall use Pannekoek's account of 'The discovery of Neptune' (1953) for purposes of illustration. In choosing this study I initially had in mind both its inherent merit and suitability, and its relationship to the earlier disussion of discovery in section 3.1. But the choice has proved doubly fortunate, since there is now hope that a properly thorough and altogether admirable ethnomethodological treatment of scientific discovery will be available by the time these words are read (Brannigan, forthcoming; cf. also Brannigan, 1979).

In the late eighteenth century the planet Uranus was 'discovered' and its orbit was studied in great detail. It was found that, after allowing for every known perturbation, the orbit none the less systematically deviated from expectation: it varied by a very small but significant amount from the predictions of classical mechanics. This led to the suggestion that a further (as yet unknown) planet existed which orbited the sun at a greater distance than Uranus itself, and affected its motion. During the 1840s two theoretical astronomers, Adams in England and Leverrier in France, calculated the orbit of the unknown planet and its current position. And in 1846, in Berlin, the prompting of Leverrier led to confirmation that a celestial object with all the characteristics of a planet was indeed to be observed within 1° of the predicted position. The object was Neptune; its discovery was, it was said, a remarkable triumph for the laws of mechanics by which its existence had been deduced and its orbit calculated.

As more details of the orbit of Neptune became available, however, the precise status of the discovery of 1846 became problematic. The 'real' and the 'predicted' orbits diverged, to the extent that it was questioned whether the one could properly count as a prediction of the other (cf. Figure 5.1). The American astronomer Peirce denied that the discovery had been made: 'Neptune is not the planet whose orbit was calculated by Leverrier and Adams but a different one which happened to be in the same neighbourhood' (Pannekoek, 1953, p. 134). Peirce, with another American astronomer, Walker, showed how assumptions in the calculations of Adams and Leverrier had led to one particular solution for the orbit; the motion of Neptune itself represented a different solution. Had Adams and Leverrier assumed a smaller over-all size of orbit, and a smaller mass for the planet, they would have produced a solution much closer to the 'real' orbit.

In Europe, however, Leverrier and Adams continued to be honoured as discoverers of Neptune, and the discovery itself continued to be accounted an instance of the predictive power of scientific laws. Nor was this position difficult to defend: the existence of a planet close to a certain point had been predicted; a planet had been found close to that point; no calculation or prediction is ever perfect.

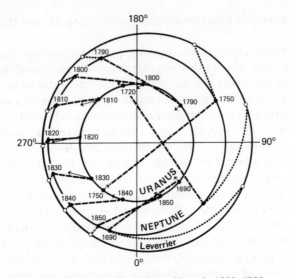

'Uranus and Neptune with their positions in 1690, 1720,
1750, 1790, 1800, etc., and the lines joining these positions.
Outside is the second orbit calculated by Leverrier (August 1846)
with the positions at the same instants. One sees that the calculated
and true positions of Neptune are close together between 1800 and 1850
but far apart during the whole of the eighteenth century.'

Source: Pannekoek (1953).

FIGURE 5.1   *The orbits of Uranus and Neptune*

At least two accounts were tenable then, and both were
employed, without logical or semantic problems, by scientists themselves. But which is the correct account? Did Leverrier and Adams
discover Neptune or did they not? These questions invite us to take
a position ourselves upon the issue. And, of course, it is perfectly
possible to do this, and then to invent arguments in favour of the
position we choose. But were we to do this, we would be doing
neither more nor less than the scientists themselves were doing in
the actual setting of the example. So if we are capable of recognising
that the 'data' (as, for example, set out in Figure 5.1) do not by their
very nature settle matters in favour of either of the opposed
accounts of the scientists, then we should be able to recognise also
that any interpretation we prefer will have no special status in relation to that 'data'. Our preferences will be a matter of how we are,
more than of how reality is.

This realignment of perception away from nature on to people is most strongly and radically undertaken by ethnomethodologists. Their methods of investigation concentrate exclusively upon discourse and communication. In the above, for example, events constitute a discovery only to the extent that it is held that events constitute a discovery. So strongly do ethnomethodologists stress this point that they sometimes formulate it as follows. The methods used to describe and account for something (e.g. discovery) are identical with that something. Thus a discovery is not an independently existing phenomenon. To talk about a discovery is to talk about talk, including the very talk that is the 'talking-about'.

[margin note: ethnom.- focus on discourse & communication.]

Accordingly, in the present example, the question is not whether or not Leverrier and Adams discovered Neptune; it is how a description of Leverrier and Adams discovering Neptune was accomplished in one setting, and a description of their failure to discover Neptune was accomplished in another setting. Similarly, for discovery generally, the ethnomethodological question is always how people succeed in displaying matters as discoveries, and the answer is always obtained by looking at the methods of accounting employed. The general approach of ethnomethodology is to explore, for any term, the methods of accounting people employ to make things visible as instances of the term. Hence ethnomethodology can be accounted the most extreme form of nominalism currently practised in the social sciences. (And if sociologists would only use terms as most other academics use them, it could be accounted the most extreme form of positivism also.)

It is important to recognise just how thoroughgoing and uncompromising is the nominalism of many ethnomethodologists. Consider again the two possible accounts of the calculations of Adams and Leverrier and the orbit of the planet Neptune. Pannekoek asks *why* one account was preferred in Europe, and the other in the USA. His answer cites distinct goals and interests associated with the two contexts. In Europe, natural science was an important component in the ideological struggles of the time. It was an alternative to the traditional religious doctrines of the established Churches and the landed classes, and was supported by an increasingly powerful and vigorous bourgeoisie. Hence it was important, for political ends, to demonstrate to as wide an audience as possible the power and scope of natural science and its laws. An account of Leverrier and Adams as successful predictors of an unknown planet fulfilled this function well. In the USA, on the other hand, there was no analogous incentive to adopt such an account, whereas by stressing the difference between the real and the predicted behaviour of the planet the American astronomers could emphasise the significance of their own technical competences.

The particular merits of this explanation of Pannekoek's do not matter here. What is interesting is his explanatory strategy. He perceives that at least two methods of accounting were possible, and he explains their association with two distinct contexts by references to goals and interests. Many sociologists would recognise this as a sound procedure. But a properly puritanical ethnomethodologist would not proceed in this way: the result of such 'positive theorising' would, from an uncompromising ethnomethodological viewpoint, not be a contribution to explanation, but merely another sample of discourse to be analysed. Just as Leverrier's work was accounted by European scientists as a prediction of Neptune's orbit, so is this accounted by Pannekoek as the consequence of goals and interests. Pannekoek's invocation of interests simply generates another account for ethnomethodological study (cf. Wieder, 1976). So similarly would any other attempt at 'positive theorising' (cf. Douglas, 1971).

In section 2.3 above it was emphasised that present proper usage is always underdetermined by previous usage. So far, however, no attempt has been made positively to build upon the point (nor is there anything in Kuhn which would help to do so). Now here are two contrasting responses to the issue. Pannekoek seeks to move closer to an adequate explanation of concept application by considering the role of interests; this is the approach I shall take up and develop in the next section. Ethnomethodologists, however, suggest that any attempt to explain specific acts of usage must be methodologically unsound: they study only methods of accounting, and refrain from asking *why* those methods are employed in one way rather than another. Some of them hold back from such 'why' questions as a matter of epistemological principle, willingly recognising that they thereby call into question every other current approach within the social sciences.

One does not, however, have to share the asceticism of ethnomethodologists to recognise the value of their actual studies, and to welcome their increasing interest in scientific discourse and in that of philosophers, historians and sociologists of science. Many of the central concepts used in the description of scientific culture merit examination from an ethnomethodological perspective. An obvious example is Kuhn's own concept of 'anomaly', which plays a key role in his account of scientific revolution. It would be fair to say that, according to Kuhn, anomalies cause revolutions even though they are not sufficient causes of them. Let us then examine more closely what we should understand by an anomaly.

According to Kuhn, awareness of anomaly is 'the recognition that nature has somehow violated the paradigm-induced expectations' (1970, p. 52). One way of interpreting this definition is to stress its social-psychological dimension. An anomaly is that which surprises people, that which goes against what they immediately predict or are prepared for. Kuhn himself stresses this aspect of anomaly when he cites the work of Bruner and Postman, who conducted psychological experiments with 'anomalous' playing-cards (1970, p. 63). Bruner and Postman found that, on a short exposure to such cards as a red six-of-spades or a black four-of-hearts, people would identify them as of some normal kind and fail to perceive any oddity. A card would be seen as a black six-of-spades, say, or a red four-of-hearts. On slightly longer exposures subjects became aware of problems and difficulties, and some became distressed by their 'anomalous' experiences. Indubitably, here is good evidence that people have strong cognitive expectations, which when confounded by natural phenomena can generate surprise and confusion.

But there is a further finding of the Bruner and Postman experiments which must not be overlooked. As exposure times were increased, subjects eventually recognised and described the red six-of-spades and the black four-of-hearts. No theories were revised; no generalisations about the nature of playing-cards were discarded. Subjects recognised some new kinds of thing and, having so recognised them, no doubt carried on as before. What subjects already knew was not in any obvious sense contradicted.

Analogously, in the case of scientists, violation of the expectations of individuals or groups could simply result in a further expectation being added to existing ones, and everything carrying on as before. A social-psychological notion of anomaly simply does not do the work required. The unexpected can always be routinely dealt with by adding a further memory to the store. If anomalies evoke crises and revolutions, the question is why those responses are preferred to more conservative alternatives; Kuhn never systematically gets to grips with this issue.

There are in any case serious objections to be faced by the standard social-psychological conception of anomaly, including some provided by Kuhn himself:

> every problem that normal science sees as a puzzle can be seen from another viewpoint, as a counterinstance and thus as a source of crisis. Copernicus saw as counterinstances what most of Ptolemy's other successors had seen as puzzles in the match between observation and theory. Lavoisier saw as a counterinstance what Priestley had seen as a successfully solved puzzle in the articulation of the phlogiston theory. And Einstein saw as counterinstances what Lorentz, Fitzgerald, and others had seen as puzzles in the articulation of Newton's and Maxwell's theories . . . either no scientific theory ever confronts a counterinstance, or all such theories confront counterinstances at all times (1970, pp. 79–80).

What one scientist sees as an anomaly another sees as a puzzle for the same paradigm — even as a successfully solved puzzle. There is an obvious analogy between the present problem of why things are accounted anomalies, and the preceding discussion of why things are accounted discoveries. If Kuhn is right here, then it is not so much that a sense of anomaly is forced upon scientists, as that they account the paradigm-reality relation a misfit as a matter of their own decision. Accordingly, it is tempting to suggest that anomalous events, rather than generating a sense of unease with paradigms, are termed anomalies to *signify* the unease which scientists feel with their paradigms. If the unease were not already felt, then terms like 'puzzle' or 'problem' would as like as not be used, or even 'solution' or 'successful prediction'.

It is entirely characteristic of Kuhn's work, backed as it is with concrete historical materials, that it should contain within itself some of the most cogent grounds and illustrations with which to call into question one of its explicit general claims. Kuhn accurately identifies the attribution of anomaly as an accounting strategy of scientists. His diagnosis in the above quotation is valid in general, and can be illustrated by any number of examples (cf. Winsor, 1976; Lakatos, 1963). But to the extent that the attribution of anomaly is an accounting strategy, anomalies cannot explain changes in the practice of research. Attributions of anomaly in science should help not to satisfy our curiosity but to stimulate it.

5.2 Goals and interests

To identify verbally articulated knowledge as a system of conventions is useful only to the extent that we understand conventional behaviour. So far, however, we have merely eliminated some possible accounts of how linguistic conventions are maintained, applied and developed. The finitist account of concept application has exposed the insufficiency of previous usage, reality, 'reason', or any combination of the three, in determining the next instance of use, or of proper use, of a term. But nothing has been said of what actually does determine the contingent judgements which develop usage. Unless we regard this as a non-problem, and adopt the avoiding strategy outlined above in section 5.1, we must accept the obligation to search further for determinants of concept application. This is what I shall do in this section, in the belief that the 'positive theorising' so offensive to some ethnomethodologists will eventually prove to have its merits after all.

The first thing to recognise, in seeking to understand concept application, is that it is futile to take verbal formulations themselves as determinants. Nothing is solved by invoking values, principles, aphorisms, metaphysical commitments, theoretical assumptions, and the like. An act of concept application cannot be explained in terms of, say, conformity to a principle, since the implications of the verbal formulation which is the principle depend upon how its constituent concepts are actively interpreted. Appeal to a verbal formulation *increases* the difficulties of explanation. This is why idealist explanations, which take concepts, ideas or beliefs as their independent variables, are fundamentally misconceived. Despite their current popularity in sociology there is no alternative but to reject them. Unless one opposes finitism, and invests concepts with intrinsic powers, one has to look beyond mere words for proper explanations (cf. also Barnes, 1977; Barnes and Mackenzie, 1979; Barnes, 1980).

What then of habit? Although concept application is never sufficiently determined by previous usage, we do as a matter of fact have no trouble in routinely applying concepts most of the time. It is as though our perception and cognition are themselves routinised, so that linguistically we operate in normal situations in an automatic manner. Should we not then explain concept application as the outcome of the habituation and routinisation of our cognitive processes? There is much to be said for this kind of explanation; but it is inadequate just as it stands. People can and do break with habit and routine; and this is part of what has to be explained. Moreover, habit in the individual does not account for an agreed application of a concept. This requires reference to social interaction, and collective understandings. Individuals must defer to authority in semantic matters.

The linguistic usage of the individual is intelligible, most of the time, as conforming behaviour, signalling the recognition of communal authority. But reference to authority is insufficient as explanation, in just the way that reference to habit is insufficient. Authority can be rejected, just as habit can be rejected; and as sufficient members reject what they perceive to be the authoritative indications of their group, those indications themselves disappear. Moreover, that authority supports one option for concept application rather than another constitutes a problem in itself: authority does not move randomly to the support of one or other option. And in asking why authority stands where it does, the entire question of the determination of concept application is confronted afresh.

Habit and authority can be taken in many cases as the immediate causes of acts of concept application, or agreement on concept application. The routinisation of linguistic usage is manifest in what is habitual at the level of the individual, and authoritative at the level of the community. Such routinisation is crucial to our use of concepts. But the nature of that routinisation must itself be understood by reference to further causes. People sustain, develop, modify or abandon their routines as they see fit, and this is as true of linguistic routines as of any other.

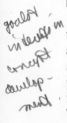

To understand concept application we must unpack the notion that people develop usage 'as they see fit'. We must turn to the goals and interests which inform judgement when concepts are applied and usage is developed. It is by reference to goals and interests that particular modes of concept application, selected from and preferred to innumerable alternative options, can be made intelligible. This was Pannekoek's approach when, as was described in the previous section, he attempted to account for opposed strategies in applying the concept 'discovery'. Whatever its specific merits, his informal explanation was of the form required.

We still lack a precise and detailed account of the relationship between goals and interests on the one hand, and concepts and beliefs on the other. For a long time yet, all discussions of this difficult issue must be tentative and provisional. None the less the fact of the relationship and a certain amount concerning its form can be asserted with confidence.

When a concept is applied, a particular is attached to one cluster of instances in preference to others. This preference must be taken to reflect a judgement as to which strategy of concept application best furthers specific goals, objectives or interests. Similarly, general acceptance of the preferred strategy reflects the shared judgement that communal goals, objectives or interests are best furthered thereby. Similarity relations develop, and knowledge grows, as whole series of such judgements are made over time, taking into account sometimes this and sometimes that constellation of goals and interests. Those goals and interests which operate the most consistently and persistently as a community employs a specific range of concepts will have the major role in determining the character of the accepted instances and generalisations routinely associated with the concepts (Barnes, 1980).

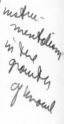

This amounts to a thoroughgoing and uncompromising instrumentalist account of the growth of knowledge. Note that goals and interests are not invoked as alternative considerations to those of truth or empirical adequacy or rationality. It is not that agents apply concepts, and evaluate the application of concepts, by referring to goals and interests instead of to criteria of, say, truth. Rather, it is that what they take to be true is intelligible only after examination of the relevant contingent goals and interests. Goals and interests have to be constituted into our basic conception of what the evaluation of knowledge requires (cf. Habermas, 1972). When esoteric, technical knowledge is encountered, like that of the physical sciences, then its use and development is intelligible in relation to specific, context-dependent technical, predictive goals and interests, rather than to abstract criteria, or 'correspondence rules', or any other verbal formulations.

But although reference to goals and interests supersedes reference to verbal rules and standards, it emphatically does not supersede reference to routines, and to the role of habit and authority.

There is a crucial relationship between goals and interests on the one hand, and routines, and hence existing knowledge, on the other. Goals and interests bear upon the judgement involved in any act of concept application. But such a judgement can only be made if *other* concepts are assumed to have a routine usage which others will continue to follow, and which can accordingly be taken for granted as a stable feature when the judgement is made. There is no way of judging the pragmatic value of continuing to use 'goose' as a term denoting a species, if in the meantime usage of the term 'species' is developing rapidly and unpredictably. Hence goals and interests, considered in the context of an over-all, coherent, verbal culture, must, for the most part, act upon judgements so that concepts are applied in the expected way, the predicted way, the way that is called 'routine'. There is a limit to the possible incongruity between habits and interests, between what is routinised and institutionalised and what is immediately indicated by reference to shared goals and objectives. Interests can completely confirm and reinforce routines, but cannot run completely against them. Interests cannot press too hard upon routine usage without counterproductive effects. The role of interests can be no more than to develop and modify an existing basis of routine. At the level of the over-all culture, goals and interests account for the relationship between old knowledge and new. Old knowledge, old routines, are necessary conditions in the understanding of the new. It is the historical development of existing bodies of knowledge which the invocation of goals and interests helps us to understand (Barnes, 1977, 1980).

There is a sense in which all the specific goals and interests associated with a form of culture are furthered by a usage which gives priority to what comes automatically and unthinkingly to its members. This usage stocks the similarity relations with shared particulars, making good the losses of particulars from the communal memory, and ensuring that the similarity relations stay shared, and that there is no degeneration towards the impossibilities that are private languages. The shared relations are the necessary prerequisites to the profitable employment of verbal culture in relation to any goal or interest whatsoever. Linguistic usage in any culture accordingly tends towards conditions of maximum cognitive laziness. Such conditions are a prerequisite for communication and information transfer, so that to further their establishment is also to further any and all more specific goals and interests.

For those who like evolutionary-functional explanations of human competences, here is a place where they can be tried. That incessant twittering of conversation which accompanies all communal activity, for all that it is often so undirected and meandering, can be given a role. It is the mechanism which has evolved to maintain tolerable overlaps of the finite clusters of instances which different individuals associate with specific terms. It maintains the communal character of similarity relations, and thus it maintains agreement in the language we use. Without this particular kind of agreement, culture ceases to be a viable instrument: we can no longer use concepts to transmit information; and hence we cannot communally develop similarity relations with reference to technical or social objectives. Such agreement has to be maintained by constant linguistic interaction, even where there is no clear-cut immediate 'need' for such interaction. To be effective learning machines, and effective inferring machines, we must be effective twittering machines (Klee, 1922).

In summary, then, the development of existing similarity relations through specific acts of concept application, and through the communal evaluation of these acts, is made more intelligible by reference to goals and interests. The remainder of the section simply seeks to consolidate and fill out this basic position. Two objectives must be paramount here. First, existing Manichaean conceptions of the role of interests as biases and distorting factors must be addressed and shown to be inadequate (cf. section 2.2). This involves considering the relationship between 'science' and 'ideology'. Second, the positive claims made above must be more concretely illustrated, and in particular it must be shown how interests are constituted into the evaluation even of esoteric, technical, predictively useful knowledge. I shall attempt to further both objectives at once by considering possible modes of use of human gender terms: two hypothetical developments of usage of 'male' and 'female' will be considered, one *prima facie* 'ideological', the other 'scientific'.

It is easy to invent a hypothetical case of the 'ideological' use of gender terms, simply by extension from existing controversies. Imagine, for example, a controversy between conservative hereditarians and liberal environmentalists, where opposed social interests sustain opposed beliefs about gender. The former group might hold that all sexual difference is the consequence of karyotype difference, that aggressiveness, for example, is higher in XY individuals because of their inherent tendency to secrete greater concentrations of certain hormones, and that males are just XY individuals. The latter group, in contrast, could say that behavioural sexual differences are learned, that differences in aggressiveness reflect differences in role definition, and that male individuals are simply those with the status of male. Were a controversy of this kind to churn endlessly on, apparently immune to inputs of 'data' as far as its basic structure was concerned, just as some actual heredity/environment controversies have continued, then we would probably accept it as a reasonable example of a clash of opposed 'ideologies', and would relate the stability of the central doctrines on the two sides to opposed socio-political interests.

It is tempting to suggest that interests operate as biases in this kind of case, and force the 'ideologies' out of conformity with experience. We already know, however, that such a position is unsatisfactory. Conceptual fabrics can always be maintained by Duhem-type strategies so that, whatever their form, they remain both internally consistent and also consistent with experience (cf. section 4.2). Hence the protagonists of hereditarian and environmentalist ideologies could indubitably keep their respective systems consistent in just this way. They could ensure that key claims were maintained, and that any adjustment to 'evidence' was made at the periphery of the conceptual fabric. Two alternative accounts of experience would be the result, both consistent and compatible with experience, but both related to broadly based socio-political interests and in that sense both 'ideologies'.

The temptation to refer to 'bias' in this kind of example arises because Manichaean mythology is the institutionalised idiom for expressing evaluations of knowledge. We examine a body of doctrine, note that it is used in the furtherance of socio-political objectives, and conjecture that its central claims are maintained only because of their relevance to those objectives. Accordingly, we (usually) form a negative evaluation of the doctrines in question. Then we turn to Manichaean myth as the normal idiom in which to *express* a negative evaluation; and we speak of bias and incompatibility with experience. This mode of speech signals our disapproval of the interests in question as relevant factors in the evaluation of knowledge. Where goals or interests of which we do approve bear upon evaluation, we do not speak of bias. For example, if specific, local technical-predictive goals and interests lead to the use and positive evaluation of such terms as 'latent heat', or such generalisations as Boyle's law, we tend not to speak of biases, even though we believe the law to be false and the term to be misleading. Although these 'scientific' concepts and generalisations are retained and used only in so far as they further contingent goals and interests, they are not explicitly spoken of in this way, since that would signal disapproval: to signal approval one speaks of nature, not culture; of correspondence with experience, not evaluation in relation to interest (cf. the discussion in Habermas, 1972, especially ch. 9 and appendix).

The development and evaluation of usage in terms of an interest in prediction and control (to borrow Habermas's term, if not precisely his concept) is something which is very widely approved and accepted, and which is accordingly spoken of simply as 'describing nature'. It is widely approved because the ability to predict and successfully intervene in natural processes is valued in all modes of life: it is the nearest thing to a universal goal or interest which makes concordance with nature the nearest thing to a universal legitimation. (Note how proponents of 'ideologies' almost always deny the role of narrow socio-political interests in determining their usage and tend to make out their doctrines as direct representations of nature.) None the less those interests of which we approve and those of which we disapprove do not bear upon the development and evaluation of usage separately and disparately, so that from a sociological perspective there is no value in a fundamental distinction between 'science' and 'ideology'.

How precisely do 'interests in prediction and control' bear upon the development of similarity relations and the evaluation of knowledge? What would it mean, for example, to claim that the usage of 'male' in a specific context over a specific period was related to an interest in prediction and control? The first step here must be to consider a generalisation including 'male'. Such a generalisation, say, 'males always secrete hormone H', can be employed for prediction, i.e. to make a guess about a future state of affairs. To be used in this way, the routine, unreflective employment of 'male' must be possible, as well as of 'hormone H': then whoever is routinely considered male will be expected to secrete a substance routinely identifiable as H — and this expectation will lead on to *prima facie* confirmations or disappointments. The more frequent is confirmation in this sense, and the less frequent disappointment in this sense, the greater is the predictive and instrumental utility of the generalisation. Where communities create, develop and modify their usage so that this kind of confirmation becomes more frequent, and this kind of disappointment less frequent, in the course of their activity, then predictive and technical-instrumental interests are served.

Were a scientific community to develop usage with special regard to the predictive utility of 'males always secrete hormone H', then it is likely that the similarity relation 'male' in that context would become progressively less distinct from the similarity relation 'XY'. 'Male' would undergo this development of usage via a series of acts of concept application evaluated in relation to a specific situated interest in prediction and control.

Another way of describing this same development is as a series of associative learning operations and inductive inferences. To sort out that cluster of instances of 'male' which maximises the predictive utility of 'males always secrete hormone H' involves proceeding inductively, on the assumption that what is most strongly associated in past experience will continue to be so in future experience. Any modification of a similarity relation designed to make a generalisation better to guess with involves and presumes the validity of this basic inductive presupposition, though we rarely take explicit note of the fact because in our cognition we are congenitally inductive. We are, as Hesse (1974) puts it, inductive learning machines (cf. also Hesse, 1980; Barnes, 1980).

On first examination, the development of the similarity relation 'male' as described above sounds fundamentally different from what would be involved in its 'ideological' development. A Manichaean might argue that the former development is guided by 'inductive logic' and the latter by social interests, and that there is a contrast to be made between 'scientific' and 'ideological' developments after all. But it is precisely because we are congenitally inductive that this contrast cannot stand. An 'ideological' development can always be accounted inductively sensible in just the way that a 'scientific' development is so accounted. For example, neither of the two 'ideologies of gender' mentioned above involve any deviation from the compelling indications of 'inductive logic'. The Duhem-type defensive strategies involved in their maintenance are themselves varieties of inductive inference. Indeed, any Duhem-type 'defensive strategy' can equally well be described as a form of learning. Imagine a hereditarian who seems to be fighting a desperate rearguard action against evidence contradicting his conception of innate male aggressiveness. He might say that he is *learning* about all the many factors which are capable of masking that innate aggressiveness. He might even offer generalisations 'good to guess with' concerning how malnutrition, fatigue, disease, etc., mask innate aggressiveness. Instead of finding inductive inference dislocated by social interests, we would find it *structured* by those interests. Even in this kind of context reasoning capabilities and social factors must be run together as codeterminants of cognition.

Conversely, just as 'ideological' developments are not related to social factors *instead* of to what is inductively indicated, so 'scientific' developments are not related to the indications of 'inductive logic' *instead* of to social considerations. I spoke above of a 'scientific' context wherein the similarity relation 'male' was developed to make the generalisation 'males always secrete hormone *H*' better to guess with. But the problem is never to make just one generalisation 'better' in this way. Similarity relations can appear in any number of generalisations, and what makes one better to guess with will invariably make some other worse. There simply is no logic to indicate how a term should be mapped on to new experience when that term is part of a whole system of terms and generalisations, i.e. when it is part of the cultural resources of an actual community. The development of the similarity relation 'male' may, for example, proceed with particular reference to generalisations about behaviour, personality, anatomy, endocrinology, or karyotype, with different outcomes resulting in each case. There is no logic to determine the relative technical advantages of the alternative strategies of concept application: people simply have to agree which generalisations they will take account of, and agree in their practice how they will be taken account of.

The form of such agreement can be different in different contexts, so that a similarity relation differentiates into several progeny, each usually (but not always) accompanied by a new verbal sign. For example, across different academic specialties the similarity relation 'male' might differentiate to give '*XY* male', '*XYY* male', 'morphological male', 'psychological male', 'male status', and so on. Such differentiation would reflect the concentration of different specialties upon different key generalisations, each

[handwritten marginal notes:] no 'logic' to force extension of term to new experience — holism embraces values & interests

bound up with a particular narrow range of procedures and competences

Why do specialties concentrate in this way, with authority and
control connecting inference predominantly to a narrow range of
generalisations and associated activities? (This comes close to asking why Kuhn's description of paradigm-sharing communities is so
apposite.) No doubt the initial processes of narrowing and concentration are susceptible of no single kind of explanation, and can
result from any number of circumstances. But once a particular
pattern has emerged, vested interests are immediately generated
which tend to maintain it. Laboriously acquired competences and
procedures are valued and not abandoned lightly; accepted laws
and definitions become emblems of prestige and standing as well as
technical resources. Thus distinct similarity relations, and strategies
of concept application, emerge in different specialties and are sustained by distinct professional vested interests. Between specialties,
these distinct strategies may be made out as compatible when co-op-
eration and alliances of expertise are the order of the day, or as contradictory and mutually inconsistent when competition and hostility
exist (cf. Mackenzie and Barnes, 1975, 1979; Dean, 1979; Latour
and Woolgar, 1979). One of the more interesting features of modern natural science is the extent to which it has achieved a *pro forma*
agreement that the beliefs and practices of its diverse specialties are
compatible as parts of a greater whole.

In any scientific specialty inference is at once inductive and
socially structured. In that inferences make generalisations better to
guess with, they relate to an 'interest in prediction and control' and
are forms of induction. In that inferences take account of some
existing generalisations rather than others, and take account of
them in a specific context of use, they relate to social interests and
are conventional. Nor is the social dimension an optional extra:
remove it and refer only to innate inductive propensities, and immediately acts of concept application and associated inferences are
insufficiently determined. No account of inductive logic, or of an
individual agent as an inductive learning machine, suffices to identify the 'best' way of applying a specific concept. The inductive
learning machine which generates and extends knowledge is a community not an individual. And what a community finds inductively
reasonable is invariably a matter of convention.

In summary, the features of both the above examples, the 'scientific' and the 'ideological', and the parallels between the examples, conclusively expose the deficiencies of Manichaean myth. Learning as a result of experience may occur in both cases; some generalisations may become better to guess with over time. An interest in prediction and control is not operative solely in a 'scientific' setting. Similarly, narrow social interests exist in both cases, bearing upon concept application and the evaluation of knowledge. Such interests are not specific to 'ideological' settings, if only because professional vested interests always inform the development of accepted usage in 'scientific' settings, narrowing the range of options to make an agreed pattern a possibility.

The discussion of the development of 'scientific' and 'ideological' usage began by asserting that interests featured in the evaluation of both. It has finished by noting that the same kinds of interest figure in both contexts. No sound basis has been found for a distinction between 'science' and 'ideology'. This is not to imply criticism of our informal intuitions. When (and if) we consider verbal utterances in relation to concrete activity, and perceive one group arguing, legitimating, advocating political programmes, whereas another is measuring, recording, analysing, experimenting, then contrasts of the scientific and the ideological make practical sense. They describe concepts and associated activities as they occur in a *context of use*; and they imply a judgement as to what goals actually predominate when usage is developed and evaluated. When we regard the development of a similarity relation as predominently bound up with technical-predictive activity we tend to talk of 'science'; where the development is seen to be mainly bound up with persuasive interaction and political activity we talk of 'ideology'. But although this is satisfactory as informal discourse, the implied distinction between different kinds of knowledge cannot stand. It is the last gasp of Manichaean mythology which would claim that science is the kind of knowledge which results from a socially structured orientation to technical or predictive goals, whereas ideology is the analogous product of social or political goals.

Goals and interests, it is crucial to remember, bear upon the collective activity of people. They help us to understand why something was done: why, for example, a concept was applied, or accepted in an application, in a specific context at a specific time. Goals and interests are not simple correlates of alleged kinds of knowledge; they are factors in the explanation of *institutional dynamics*.

In their total impact upon us as organisms they induce us to develop or change our concepts and generalisations from their state at an earlier point of time (cf. Figure 5.2). Hence that earlier stage of our knowledge and culture must always be a necessary element in the explanation of any later state (Barnes, 1977, 1980).

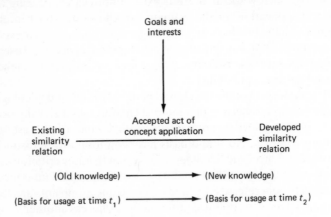

FIGURE 5.2　*Interests and the growth of knowledge*

To grasp what the growth of knowledge consists in, one must take the form of the act of concept application and iterate it in the imagination on a grand scale. Whole communities must be considered over a period of time, incessantly clustering particulars and developing similarity relations. On all this multitude of acts of concept application goals and interests will make their impact, sometimes in one configuration and sometimes in another, sometimes with one effect and sometimes with another, as the over-all historical development proceeds. There is no way of asserting a correspondence between a concept or a belief, and a specific kind of objective or interest, once the character of this historical sequence is recognised.

A similarity relation is the product of the usage of a specific term. It is built up from a sequence of acts of concept application. But in that sequence all kinds of goals and interests may well have had a bearing. And we can never hope fully to confirm the pedigree of any relation before we use it ourselves. When we talk of particular similarity relations, or of the generalisations wherein they function, as parts of science, we must recognise this as no more than the expression of a conventional attitude. No doubt it will reflect the fact that the relation has been received from the ancestors within a specific context of use. But it should not be taken as an imputation of any particular properties to the relation itself. Unfortunately, when we refer to a part of culture as 'science' or 'ideology' (or 'religion' or 'philosophy'), this last, incorrect form of understanding is frequently predominant, and gives rise to endless confusions. We imagine that 'science', 'ideology', etc., can be described in terms of inherent properties, and we offer 'theories' which do this. And whatever the theories are, we thereby create for ourselves disturbing historical spectacles such as those of 'ideology' transforming itself into 'science', or 'science' and 'metaphysics' metamorphosing back and forth into each other. These mysterious historical transformations of ideas threaten to paralyse the mind until we realise that we are simply looking at people changing the modes of use to which they put their culture.

Turning to the present, similarity relations remain, as always, nothing more than clusters of instances. How they are next extended is a matter for their users. The relations do not include instructions concerning their mode of use, or what goals and interests are to be taken into account as they are developed. As clusters, the relations have no properties other than that of being clusters. They are inert: available for that usage wherein they are used; a resource for those willing to take them as a resource. Hence we should always think, not of different kinds of knowledge and culture, but of different modes of use of the knowledge and culture which we share.

Finitism and instrumentalism are complementary and mutually reinforcing. To the extent that concepts are imbued with inherent powers and properties a limitation is set upon an instrumentalist account of the growth of knowledge. Conversely, a finitist account of concept application can never amount to an *explanation*, unless it is supplemented by some reference to contingent goals and interests. The value of the finitist analysis itself is largely negative: it undermines a wide range of highly favoured but misconceived philosophical and sociological doctrines, and thereby prepares the way for something better. But if a positive understanding of concept application is sought, then it is necessary to step out beyond finitism, and search for the causes of situated human activity. A close reading of Kuhn's work brings home this point vividly. His analysis effectively undermines most orthodox rationalisations of scientific investigation and inference. The emptiness of so many references to 'reason', 'rational justification', 'logic', 'proof', 'experience', 'reality', etc., is exposed. And the conventional character of scientific judgement is clearly delineated. Kuhn provides everything which can reasonably be expected of a finitist account of knowledge (even though he himself never explicitly identifies his account as of this kind). But when one searches for positive explanations in Kuhn's work, one rapidly becomes aware of a sense of dissatisfaction. *Why* does a new problem-solution become communally accepted as a problem-solution? *Why* is it counted as an extension of an existing paradigm, as the same as what has gone before? *Why* can one man's successful problem-solution be another man's anomaly? And *why* are those on opposite sides in controversies concerning alternative paradigms to be found on those alternative sides? To these and many similar questions Kuhn's work provides no satisfactory answers. It cannot do so because it never systematically takes into account the profoundly purposive, goal-oriented character of all human activity and cognition. None the less Kuhn allows us to see the depth of these questions, and the vacuity of most existing answers to them: his work sweeps up the debris of what used to be an unduly pervasive philosophical tradition, and that is achievement enough.

5.3   Science in context

If the preceding arguments are correct, then inferences and judgements in science are always structured by contingent features of the settings wherein they occur, and in particular by communal goals and interests. To understand judgements in a specific community one must address its activity, the resources available for that activity, and the communal goals towards the attainment of which activity is directed. Depending upon the particular case studied, these communal goals and resources may be specific to the immediate context, the narrow realm of the differentiated scientific subculture; or they may be much more widely diffused. Narrow professional vested interests may help to account for how inference proceeds, or more broadly based socio-political interests may. But in either case the way in which interests structure inference, and hence the way in which judgements are explained, will be formally the same.

Since there are now several empirical studies which attempt to relate scientific knowledge and interests, these points can be made more concretely. Forman (1971) has attempted to relate the ready acceptance by German physicists of an *acausally* interpreted quantum mechanics to general social and political conditions in the Weimar republic which made for aversion to determinism: here, the hypothesis is that broadly based social interests and objectives had a role in structuring inference. Pickering (1981) has attempted to relate the wide acceptance of the 'charm' hypothesis in modern particle physics to very specific goals and objectives located within physics itself: here, the hypothesis is that narrow professional interests structured inference, and no attention is focused upon the wider social setting. But the forms of Pickering's and Forman's very different attempts at explanation are the same. Goals and interests exist; they channel inference and judgement; they thus help to account for the emergence of a specific body of knowledge. (Nor is it self-evident that the operation of macro-political factors, as in the first case, is inherently less desirable than the operation of micro-political factors, as in the second case.)

The same points apply with regard to scientific controversies. The differing judgements of scientists in controversy have sometimes been accounted for by macro-political conditions and general social interests (cf. MacKenzie and Barnes, 1975, 1979, on the Biometry–Mendelism controversy; Farley, 1977, on the spontaneous generation controversy; MacKenzie, 1978, on controversy in statistics; Shapin, 1979, on nineteenth-century cerebral anatomy, among others). But reference to contingencies peculiar to the subculture of science can suffice to account for differences in scientific judgements upon parallel lines, with vested interests substituting for broader social interests, the esoteric context for the whole society, micro-political considerations for macro (cf. Dean, 1979, on botanical taxonomy; Pickering, forthcoming, on free (unbound) quarks). We are not dealing with different kinds of explanation here.

How far inference and evaluation in science relate to contingencies in the narrow scientific setting, and how far to macro-sociological factors, is a straightforward empirical matter. Since both kinds of contingency may operate in any specific case, separately or together, there is a need to search for both in any concrete empirical or historical study. It is unsound to assume that where one set of contingencies is operative, the other is not, that scientific judgement must relate either to narrow professional considerations or to general social considerations. It may relate to both. A recent study by Wynne (1979) is as good a model as any of what is needed. Wynne shows how the concept of the 'ether' played an important role in the laboratory culture of late-Victorian Cambridge physics. It was a technical-theoretical notion, routinely employed as experiments were designed and laws and generalisations evaluated. Motions in the 'luminiferous ether' could account for the existence of light, electricity, radiant energy and even ponderable matter. But Wynne points to another context of use wherein many of the Cambridge physicists deployed the ether concept. The term was put to work to rebut the narrowly instrumental doctrines of scientific naturalism, which were at that time being employed to assail the pretensions of establishment clerics and divines, and hence the predominance of the old landed aristocratic interest which they represented. As a scientifically useful concept which was none the less 'metaphysical' and a step beyond appearances, the ether could be pointed to to confound the naturalists. Moreover, as a theoretical entity whose properties explained such a vast range of phenomena, the ether served as the basis for a vision of a harmonious unified cosmos which by its very integration pointed beyond itself to something transcendental.

Wynne documents the use of the ether concept in the narrow, technically oriented context, and in the broader political context, and thus he shows how the concept was developed and elaborated in relation to two clusters of goals and interests at the same time. Nothing in Wynne's account justifies our setting one context before the other, one set of interests above the other. It is misleading to talk of a 'scientific' concept being used outside science, or of an 'unscientific' or 'ideological' concept being used inside. The ether concept developed by usage in two contexts of discourse. And any particular case of its use within either context could build upon previous usage in both, so that an interaction came to occur between the esoteric and the exoteric culture.

We should always assume such interaction when a scientific community is studied, and seek to ascertain its nature and intensity; zero intensity should simply count as a possible empirical finding. It is true that scientists themselves try to insulate their esoteric culture from the 'outside'; but whether and how far they succeed is an empirical matter, nothing more. In many cases it is irresistibly convenient to talk of the boundaries of a scientific field; but such talk is of a pattern people have managed to generate in their activity, not of something which determines their activity, still less of a great divide between good and evil.

A scientific sub-culture, with its own esoteric procedures, competences, objectives and standards, is just like any other. Take painting, for example. One can study the way in which people maintain the art of painting as a separate tradition, and distinguish its methods and productions from anything to be found in the wider society. At the same time, one can observe how the products of the painter's art emerge from the studios into the wider society and are put to use, as sources of simple pleasure, as decoration, as status symbols, as messages about the moral order, as statements about man's place in the world. And one can document, too, how these different requirements feed back into the esoteric painterly culture, stimulating new products, and hence new techniques and new standards. The study of painting along these lines is a routine matter which has no automatic evaluative implications. If artists respond to a demand for altarpieces, or for prestige extravaganzas, and consequently modify their methods, sensibilities and standards of judgement, it is not assumed that by virtue of that very fact they have devalued their art. This is how things should stand also in the empirical study of science, and increasingly it is how they do stand.

Admittedly, a significant residue of sociological and historical work rejects this view, and, in keeping with the requirements of the Manichaean myth of knowledge, legislates a strong boundary between science and its social context. Scientific judgement is held to proceed entirely by reference to timeless, universal 'rules of reason'. The role of social contingencies is denied, lest, as forces of darkness, they undermine the standing of scientific knowledge. Great effort is expended upon protecting science from the threats of pollution which empirical studies of its development invariably present.

In sociology the resulting image of a ship of reason powering its own one way through a silent sea of social contingencies serves merely to discourage the study of scientific knowledge and judgement. Its significance is predominantly a negative one (although a Procrustean attempt to fit actual findings to it can be found in Ben-David, 1971). Within the mainstream of the history of science, on the other hand, the Manichaean myth is more intimately woven into the fabric of both rhetoric and research. It sustains the well-known stereotypes of 'internal' and 'external' history. To do internal history is to explain scientific change by reference to the forces of light within the esoteric scientific context — observation, experiment and rational inference. To do external history involves invoking such dark outside agencies as interests and social biases for the same explanatory task. The two approaches are regarded as incompatible, the former being the ideal, and the latter the *bête noire* of much historiographical rhetoric.

Fortunately, however, the internal/external dichotomy, long a source of dissatisfaction (Thackray, 1970), is no longer of major methodological significance in the history of science, though the terms continue in use as convenient indicators of the pragmatically selected foci of particular pieces of research. Nor is there any longer a lack of empirical studies relating scientific judgement (as part of the over-all activity of research) to the wider context. Among many examples are Young (1969), Forman (1971), Thackray (1974), Brown (1974), Farley (1977), Jacob (1977), Caneva (1978), Barnes and Shapin (1979), and Shapin (1980 and forthcoming). We even have studies of the work of individual scientists which pay no regard to Manichaean myth but proceed in a thoroughly contextual and genuinely historical way (Cowan, 1977; MacKenzie, 1979). More important, however, than this trend in itself is the way that the history of science taken as a whole now offers a much broader and richer characterisation of its subject. Individual historians will disagree. Nor will any one of them ever be equally sensitive to everything in the panorama he confronts. But the very diversity of historical contributions now serves to provide an adequate account of scientific culture as it actually operates in particular social settings. (Curiously, Kuhn's latest publications have contributed remarkably little to this account. His abstract historiography always treats science as a sub-culture with conventionally drawn boundaries (Kuhn, 1968, 1971a, 1971b). But his empirical research has increasingly moved away from these boundaries, until in his most recent work on physical theory (1978) they are scarcely apparent at all.)

This broadening of perspectives in the history of science suggests

that its findings will become of increasing general sociological interest. Already, for example, there are indications that very broadly *social*
based social and political developments may be much more *impact*
intimately connected with cultural change in science than had been *on*
previously recognised, and that the role of such developments may *science –*
be particularly marked at times of major theoretical reorientation. *Darwin*
Consider, for example, the work of the two acknowledged giants of *&*
English science, Newton and Darwin, which, in both cases, has *Newton*
received extraordinarily detailed concerted historical study. The
theories of both of these men were, to say the least, closely intertwined with the explicitly political doctrines of Newtonianism and
Social Darwinism (cf. Jacob, 1976; and Shapin, 1980, for Newtonianism; Young, 1969, 1973, for Darwinism). The days have long
gone by when these associations could be characterised as 'social
misuse of scientific knowledge'. Newton's *Principia* and Darwin's
Origin possessed simultaneously a technical-instrumental and a
socio-political utility, and there is no historically reputable case for
taking the one utility to exclude the other. Wynne's comments on
the concept of the ether, outlined above, apply equally to the
notions of the inertness and paucity of matter and the role of spirit-
ual agency in Newton, and to the notions of struggle for existence
and natural selection in Darwin.

Concepts such as these, readily imbued with cosmological and
ontological significance, do appear to attain particular prominence
in the course of many of those changes which Kuhn identifies as
revolutions. Given the utility of such concepts in polemic, and their
indirect relationship with the technical tasks of the sciences, one is
bound to wonder whether 'revolutions', for all that they are primarily reorientations of esoteric practice, might not in many cases
have been stimulated or facilitated by very general socio-political
developments. Certainly, there can be few instances where historians can say with confidence that this was not so, whereas many
further cases could be cited to parallel the two above. The significance of the debate between materialists and their opponents in
itself ensures no shortage of example from the history of biology, or
from the history of theories of matter, which spans a great range of
physical science.

More historical research is needed before discussion of this
matter can be taken further. Present findings do, however, clearly
indicate the inadvisability of taking Kuhn's basic account, which

relates 'revolution' entirely to the esoteric context, as a sufficient one (cf. also Frankel, 1976).

5.4   The basis of community

I said in Chapter 1 that the sociological value of Kuhn's work extended beyond the context of natural science, and that it merited the attention of any social scientist with an interest in culture and cognition. I did not have it in mind, however, to defend the widespread use of Kuhn's ideas as a pre-packed system. The popularity of debates about whether sociology has a paradigm, or whether there have been scientific revolutions in economics or in psychology, attests more to the prevalence of intellectual laziness than to the significance of Kuhn's thinking. He himself has rightly enjoined caution in the application of his characteristic concepts, and has stressed that a case for their utility has only been made in the context of the history of the natural sciences (cf. Kuhn, 1969).

In my judgement the general significance of Kuhn's work lies neither in its specific historical narrative of the development of science, nor in the concepts invented for that narrative, but simply in its explicit discussions of general problems concerning cognition, semantics and culture. Kuhn is important where he examines similarity relations, concrete problem-solutions, and the development of usage and procedure by analogy and direct modelling. Here, our understanding of the conventional nature of knowledge is advanced, as is our understanding of the nature of convention itself. This is material which no one in the social sciences should pass over, even if Kuhn himself has not advertised its general importance.

I shall cite only one example to illustrate the potential value of Kuhn's work to sociological theory; but the example concerns a crucial question, and if it is well conceived it will suffice. First, I must recap how Kuhn seeks to understand a scientific theory. In the *Structure* he displays those holding a theory as the possessors of a number of accepted problem-solutions; and he shows how normal research consists in the extension of the problem-solutions to further cases by direct modelling. Nothing is described independent of or over and above this. It is by the competent use of paradigms that scientists acquire a sense of the meanings of terms, the implications of laws and generalisations, and hence the content of theories.

Theories are not separate from paradigms. On the contrary, a theory can be understood simply as a cluster of accepted problem-solutions. Established knowledge covers all cases routinely and unproblematically accepted as 'the same' as standard, solved problems. Current research concerns itself with cases thought to be 'the same' as standard cases but not yet decisively established as 'the same' by the development of the standard cases. A cluster of accepted problem-solutions accordingly represents both what counts as the established knowledge associated with a theory, and what is available as a resource in the development and extension of the theory.

To identify a theory as a cluster of problem-solutions is, if correct, of considerable importance. Normally we think of a theory as one thing, a system of statements perhaps, or a formal mathematical structure, from which particular solutions are deduced or logically derived. Specific problem-solutions are regarded as applications of a general theory: they are each thought to incorporate some part of the general structure of a theory itself, which is indeed why they are called applications of that theory. But now the tables are turned, and a theory, rather than defining its applications by being present in them and thereby making them 'the same', is defined by its applications: it is simply the cluster of what are called its applications.

This is not to say that all the 'applications of a theory' are completely unconnected and independent. Many resemblances are always to be found among the instances in such a cluster: a few physical constants, for example, appear again and again in most of the paradigms of classical mechanics; and specific values of pragmatically chosen quantities like the mass of the earth appear in many. But overlapping resemblances do not imply the presence of a basic logical structure, or form, or essence, 'within', 'behind' or 'above' any application of a theory. There is no more need to postulate this than there is to postulate an essence of 'duck' or 'goose'.

Stegmüller's set-theoretical account of the character of a scientific theory is inspired by and closely resembles Kuhn's informal description. It is an extremely useful account which draws attention to many of the finitist implications of Kuhn's work, and which recognises that a theory cannot be identified as something independent of its applications. But Stegmüller none the less insists that every theory possesses a basic mathematical structure and that applications are derived from the 'specialisation' of the basic structure (Stegmüller, 1976, pp. 109–10 and cf. pp. 43–4). Unfortunately, however, although his knowledge of actual science is unusually detailed for a set-theorist, Stegmüller fails to find any compelling indications of the presence of fundamental mathematical structures therein, or of the process of 'specialisation' whereby paradigms and problem-solutions are derived from such structures. Stegmüller would like to establish the existence of a level of theory above that of paradigms and problem-solutions, but his inability to do so merely tends to confirm the absence of any such level.

By postulating the existence of a basic mathematical structure of a theory, set above the clusters of applications in Kuhn's account, Stegmüller envisages something which is too close in form to the traditional deductivist view of science. A general structure, an essence more or less, is set above particular applications. An application is a 'specialisation' derived from the general structure. Inference flows down a hierarchy from the general to the particular. Particular solutions are derived from general relationships, much as deductive logicians would have it. In contrast, Kuhn's account permits the role of deduction to be called into question. A theory is presented simply as a cluster of related applications. How, then, can a deduction be made from the theory to a standard application, if the application is itself part of what the theory is? And how can non-standard applications be deduced when they are significantly different from old ones?

Scientific inference, like empirical inference generally, is not deductive. It proceeds from particular to particular on the basis of resemblance and analogy. Knowledge is built up and extended a bit at a time by the revisable clustering of instances and applications. Our sense of the scope and validity of a general claim arises from the way we develop analogies between particulars, and cluster the particulars together. Inferences, and convictions of validity, can move from particular to particular, or upwards from the particular to the general; but they cannot flow directly down the hierarchy from the general to the particular. This is because the only way to ascertain whether a general claim applies to a given particular is to consider what analogy exists between the particular and other particulars already acknowledged to be covered by the generalisation. *Any 'deduction' about empirical phenomena involves a hidden analogical step.*

Just as the relationship of the particular and the general must be faced in epistemology and the sociology of knowledge, so must it be also in the mainstream of sociological theory with regard to the explanation of action. Many sociologists, particularly those of the functionalist school, account for action by assuming the possibility of secure inference from the general to the particular. They construct a hierarchy running from 'values' to 'implied norms' and thence to the actions appropriate in specific contexts. Values are the key to the understanding of actions; they are the basis of community. Hence we have the familiar stress in functionalist theory upon the 'dominant values' of a society or institution. Others reject this position, and suggest that it is rather we ourselves who in every particular case make out actions as in conformity with norms, and make out norms as embodiments of values. This view, long espoused by symbolic interactionists and interpretative sociologists, presents the general as generated from the particular, and has inference flowing through the cognitive hierarchy in the opposite direction to that assumed by the functionalists.

To decide between these opposed views is not an easy matter; but there is perhaps no single issue of greater importance anywhere in sociological theory, and it is sad to note how often it has been ignored. The functionalist school, which until recent years has been overwhelmingly predominant in sociology, must surely carry most of the responsibility for this. At some point functionalism seems to have lost much of its original intellectual impetus, and to have allowed its theory to degenerate into a mere way of speaking. The more functionalists have talked of values and norms, the less they have troubled to convey, or even perhaps to understand, what it is that they are talking about. Interest in the real sociological questions surrounding the terms has lapsed. (There are those who spare no effort in creating and displaying analogies between sociology and the natural sciences, and who defend functionalism as the sociological paradigm. But if this allows the superficiality of late rococo functionalism to be excused as normal research, it equally allows the embarrassing question as to what puzzles functionalism has solved and what anomalies it recognises. There is much to be said for avoiding explicit analogies between the social and the natural sciences, save perhaps if we wish to chart the desert in sociology.)

The significance of values remains undecided within sociological theory. And although it has received considerable attention in recent years, and a great deal of clarification has been achieved, there is still cause to welcome any new vantage-point upon the problem. That Kuhn's work offers exactly this is immediately evident when we recognise the analogy between values and theories, actions and applications. The concepts with which we convey normative notions cannot be taught in ways fundamentally different from those employed to teach empirical concepts. In the latter case finite clusters of states of affairs are produced, in the former finite clusters of approved modes of action. And just as the most general of empirical-scientific notions, the theory as a whole, remains a finite cluster, so will the most general of normative notions, the value, remain also a finite cluster. As a theory is a cluster of accepted concrete applications, a value is a cluster of accepted modes of action — or rather, this is the most that a value can be, if it is held to be more than a mere verbal formulation.

To the extent that the analogy is accepted, the inceptive role of values in social life must be called into question. One can no more deduce an appropriate action from a value than one can deduce an application from the abstract structure of an empirical theory. Any general sense of value must be maintained by the continuing, active, revisable clustering of particular instances. Values must be the products of communal activity, not part of the basis of community. This, of course, is close to the traditional stance of symbolic interactionism, interpretative sociologies, and related finitist theories. Thus Kuhn's work gives inductive support, via the above analogy, to the various finitist schools in sociology; and its methods and concepts could, if required, pass across by the same route to become resources for a wide range of sociological research. Since finitism is now reasonably well established in sociology, this last possibility is well worth examining. It is now widely recognised that a sense of social order is built up piecemeal and sustained by a series of particular transactions; but how precisely this is accomplished remains obscure. In 1973 Cicourel summarised the position in relation to the theory of socialisation:

> The moment-to-moment programming each member accomplishes for himself and others re-establishes the normative order because of *post hoc* linking with general policies or rules. In attempting to socialise children this as yet ambiguous process of linking particular cases with general policies or rules becomes a perpetual laboratory for discovering how social organisation is

made possible through the child's acquisition of social structure (1973, p. 73).

Cicourel's book conveys very well the importance of this *post hoc* process, as well as revealing just how very little of it we understand. Kuhn's account of puzzle-solving in science, with its stress on similarity relations, modelling and analogy, and the finitist approach to scientific culture which his work has encouraged, are both potentially valuable resources with which to attack this problem. Although scientific culture may be in some ways more complex than that of children, in other ways it is simpler and easier to understand, so that there is something to be said for the methods and findings of either context also being used as resources in the other (cf. Kuhn's own use of Piaget).

It is true that Kuhn is himself both an exponent and an advocate of sociological functionalism. As such, he would scarcely be likely to agree with my analysis in this section, and there are indeed clear statements in his own work which stand in explicit opposition to what I have just written. In a lecture on 'Objectivity, Value-Judgement and Theory Choice', delivered in 1973, Kuhn stresses his conviction that values, though they may not determine action, none the less guide and influence it (1977, ch. 13; cf. also the reiteration of his position on pp. 21–2). Values, apparently, possess inherent implications and inherent potency: 'Improving the quality of life is a value, and a car in every garage once followed from it as a norm' (Kuhn, 1977, p. 330); 'there are other societies with other values and . . . these value differences result in other ways of life' (Kuhn, 1977, p. 331).

Needless to say, my own view is that this analysis of the role of values is completely incorrect, and sits most uncomfortably alongside the rest of Kuhn's work. Fortunately, however, it does not figure large in his research. He has never directed any empirical investigation to the question of the role of values in science, and he has not considered the technical ramifications of the question, or the difficulties which his own point of view has encountered in the context of the social sciences. 'Objectivity, Value-Judgement and Theory Choice' addresses issues rarely touched upon in Kuhn's other work.

Hence, if Kuhn is indeed incorrect in his appraisal of the role of values, it should count as but a small matter in the evaluation of his work. In the abstract, it is a major issue. But the significance of a body of writing has not a great deal to do with its abstract verbal formulations, even upon major issues. Marx and Durkheim have both made invaluable contributions to sociology; but the majority of all their statements are now routinely taken to be erroneous. Their value lies in the prototype methods and procedures they provide, embedded in analyses of specific situations and events. They offer resources for sociological research, not correct instructions. Perhaps the same should be said of Kuhn.

Bibliography

Allison, P. D. (1979) 'Experimental Parapsychology as a Rejected Science', *Sociological Review Monograph*, no. 27, pp. 271—92.

Barnes, S. B. (1974) *Scientific Knowledge and Sociological Theory*, London, Routledge & Kegan Paul.

Barnes, S. B. (1976) 'Natural Rationality: a Neglected Concept in the Social Sciences', *Philosophy of the Social Sciences*, vol. 6, no. 2, pp. 115—26.

Barnes, S. B. (1977) *Interests and the Growth of Knowledge*, London, Routledge & Kegan Paul.

Barnes, S. B. (1980) 'On the Conventional Character of Knowledge and Cognition', *Kölner Zeitschrift für Soziologie*, Special Edition No. 23, pp. 163—90. Also in *Philosophy of the Social Sciences*, vol. 11, no. 3, 1981.

Barnes, S. B. and Mackenzie, D. (1979) 'On the Role of Interests in Scientific Change', *Sociological Review Monograph*, no. 27, pp. 49—66.

Barnes, S. B. and Shapin, S. (eds) (1979) *Natural Order*, London, Sage.

Ben-David, J. (1971) *The Scientist's Role in Society*, Englewood Cliffs, N.J., Prentice-Hall.

Bloor, D. C. (1973) 'Wittgenstein and Mannheim on the Sociology of Mathematics', *Studies in the History and Philosophy of Science*, vol. 4, no. 2, pp. 173—91.

Bloor, D. C. (1976) *Knowledge and Social Imagery*, London, Routledge & Kegan Paul.

Brannigan, A. (1979) 'The Reification of Mendel', *Social Studies of Science*, vol. 9, no. 4, pp. 423—54.

Brannigan, A. (forthcoming) 'The Social Basis of Scientific Discovery'.

Brown, T. M. (1974) 'From Mechanism to Vitalism in Eighteenth-Century English Physiology', *Journal of the History of Biology*, vol. 7, pp. 179—216.

Caneva, K. L. (1978) 'From Galvanism to Electrodynamics: the Transformation of German Physics and its Social Context', *Historical Studies in the Physical Sciences*, vol. 9, pp. 63—160.

Cicourel, A. (1973) *Cognitive Sociology*, Harmondsworth, Penguin.

Collins, H. M. (1975) 'The Seven Sexes: a Study in the Sociology of a Phenomenon, or the Replication of Experiments in Physics', *Sociology*, vol. 9, pp. 205—24.

Collins, H. M. (1981) 'The Social Destruction of Gravitational Radiation', *Social Studies of Science*, vol. 11, no. 1, pp. 33—62.

Collins, H. M. and Pinch, T. J. (1979) 'The Construction of the Paranormal: Nothing Unscientific is Happening', in *On the Margins of Science*, ed. Wallis (1979) pp. 237—70.

Collins, H. M. and Pinch, T. J. (forthcoming) 'Science and the Spoon Benders'.

Cowan, R. S. (1977) 'Nature and Nurture: the Interplay of Biology and Politics in the Work of Francis Galton', *Studies in the History of Biology*, vol. 1, pp. 133—208.

Dean, J. (1979) 'Controversy over Classification: a Case Study from the History of Botany', in *Natural Order*, ed. Barnes and Shapin (1979).

Douglas, J. D. (1971) *Understanding Everyday Life*, London, Routledge & Kegan Paul.

Douglas, M. (1973) *Rules and Meanings*, Harmondsworth, Penguin.

Duhem, P. (1954) *The Aim and Structure of Physical Theory* (translated by P. P. Wiener from French), Princeton University Press.

Edge, D. O. and Mulkay, M. (1976) *Astronomy Transformed*, New York, Wiley.

Farley, J. (1977) *The Spontaneous Generation Controversy from Descartes to Oparin*, Baltimore, Johns Hopkins University Press.

Fleck, L. (1935) *Entstehung und Entwicklung einer Wissenschaftliche Tatsache* (English translation F. Bradley and T. J. Trenn), published as *Genesis and Development of a Scientific Fact*, University of Chicago Press, in 1979.

Forman, P. (1971) 'Weimar Culture, Causality and Quantum Theory, 1918—1927', *Historical Studies in the Physical Sciences*, vol. 3, pp. 1—115.

Frankel, E. (1976) 'Corpuscular Optics and the Wave Theory of Light', *Social Studies of Science*, vol. 6, pp. 141—84.

Frankel, H. (1979) 'The Career of Continental Drift Theory', *Studies in the History and Philosophy of Science*, vol. 10, no. 1, pp. 21—66.

Garfinkel, H. (1967) *Studies in Ethnomethodology*, Englewood Cliffs, N.J., Prentice-Hall.

Gay, H. (1976) 'Radicals and Types', *Studies in the History and Philosophy of Science*, vol. 7, pp. 1—51.

Grazia, A. de (ed.) (1966) *The Velikovsky Affair*, New York, University Books.

Habermas, J. (1972) *Knowledge and Human Interests*, London, Heinemann.

Hesse, M. B. (1974) *The Structure of Scientific Inference*, London, Macmillan.

Hesse, M. B. (1980) *Revolutions and Reconstructions in the Philosophy of Science*, Brighton, Harvester Press.

Jacob, J. R. (1977) *Robert Boyle and the English Revolution*, New York, Burt Franklin.

Jacob, M. C. (1976) *The Newtonians and the English Revolution*, Brighton, Harvester Press.

Jarvie, I. C. (1979) 'Laudan's Problematic Progress and the Social Sciences', *Philosophy of the Social Sciences*, vol. 9, pp. 484—97.

Klee, P. (1922) *The Twittering Machine*, New York, Museum of Modern Art.

Kuhn, T. S. (1955) 'Carnot's Version of "Carnot's Cycle"', *American Journal of Physics*, vol. 23, pp. 91—5.

Kuhn, T. S. (1957) *The Copernican Revolution*, Harvard University Press.

Kuhn, T. S. (1959) 'The Essential Tension', in *Third University of Utah Conference on the Identification of Scientific Talent*, ed. C. W. Taylor, University of Utah Press (reprinted in Kuhn, 1977).

Kuhn, T. S. (1960) 'Engineering Precedent for the Work of Sadi Carnot', *Archives Internationales d'Histoire des Sciences*, vol. 13, pp. 251—5.

Kuhn, T. S. (1961a) 'The Function of Measurement in Modern Physical Science', *Isis*, vol. 52, pp. 161—90 (reprinted in Kuhn, 1977).

Kuhn, T. S. (1961b) 'Sadi Carnot and the Cagnard Engine', *Isis*, vol. 52, pp. 367—74.

Kuhn, T. S. (1962) 'The Historical Structure of Scientific Discovery', *Science*, vol. 136, pp. 760—4 (reprinted in Kuhn, 1977).

Kuhn, T. S. (1963) 'The Function of Dogma in Scientific Research', in *Scientific Change*, ed. A. C. Crombie, London, Heinemann, pp. 347—69.

Kuhn, T. S. (1964) 'A Function for Thought Experiments', in *Mélanges Alexandre Koyré*, Paris, Hermann, vol. 2, pp. 307—34 (reprinted in Kuhn, 1977).

Kuhn, T. S. (1968) 'The History of Science', *International Encyclopedia of the Social Sciences*, vol. 14, pp. 74—83 (reprinted in Kuhn, 1977).

Kuhn, T. S. (1969) 'Comment on the Relations of Science and Art', *Comparative Studies in Society and History*, vol. 11, pp. 403—12 (reprinted in Kuhn, 1977).

Kuhn, T. S. (1970) *The Structure of Scientific Revolutions*, 2nd edn, University of Chicago Press (first published in 1962).

Kuhn, T. S. (1971a) 'History and the History of Science', *Daedalus*, vol. 100, pp. 271—304 (reprinted in Kuhn, 1977).

Kuhn, T. S. (1971b) 'Scientific Growth: Reflections on Ben-David's "Scientific Role"', *Minerva*, vol. 10, pp. 166—78.

Kuhn, T. S. (1974) 'Second Thoughts on Paradigms', in *The Structure of Scientific Theories*, ed. F. Suppe, Illinois University Press, pp. 459—82 (reprinted in Kuhn, 1977).

Kuhn, T. S. (1975) 'A Formalism for Scientific Change' (lecture mimeo), reprinted in *Proceedings of the International Congress of Logic, Methodology and Philosophy of Science*, ed. R. E. Butts and K. J. J. Hintikka, Reidel, 1977.

Kuhn, T. S. (1977) *The Essential Tension*, University of Chicago Press.

Kuhn, T. S. (1978) *Black Body Theory and the Quantum Discontinuity, 1894—1912*, Oxford, Clarendon Press.

Lakatos, I. (1963) 'Proofs and Refutations', *British Journal for the Philosophy of Science*, vol. 14, pp. 1—25, 120—39, 221—45, 296—342.

Lakatos, I. (1970) 'Falsification and the Methodology of Scientific Research Programmes', in *Criticism and the Growth of Knowledge*, ed. Lakatos and Musgrave (1970).

Lakatos, I. and Musgrave, A. (eds) (1970) *Criticism and the Growth of Knowledge*, Cambridge University Press.

Latour, B. and Woolgar, S. (1979) *Laboratory Life: the Social Construction of Scientific Facts*, London, Sage.

Law, J. (1975) 'Is Epistemology Redundant?', *Philosophy of the Social Sciences*, vol. 5, pp. 317—37.

Lemaine, G., MacLeod, R., Mulkay, M. and Weingart, P. (eds) (1976) *Perspectives on the Emergence of Scientific Disciplines*, The Hague, Mouton.

MacKenzie, D. (1978) 'Statistical Theory and Social Interests: a Case Study', *Social Studies of Science*, vol. 8, pp. 35—83.

MacKenzie, D. (1979) 'Karl Pearson and the Professional Middle Class', *Annals of Science*, vol. 36, pp. 125—43.

MacKenzie, D. and Barnes, S. B. (1975) 'Biometrician versus Mendelian: a Controversy and its Explanation' *Kölner Zeitschrift für Soziologie*, Special Edition No. 18, pp. 165—96.

MacKenzie, D. and Barnes, S. B. (1979) 'Scientific Judgement: the Biometry—Mendelism Controversy', in *Natural Order*, ed. Barnes and Shapin (1979).

Martin, M. (1971) 'Referential Variance and Scientific Objectivity', *British Journal for the Philosophy of Science*, vol. 22, pp. 17—26.

Masterman, M. (1970) 'The Nature of the Paradigm', in *Criticism and the Growth of Knowledge*, ed. Lakatos and Musgrave (1970) pp. 59—89.

Mullins, N. C. (1972) 'The Development of a Scientific Specialty: the Phage Group and the Origins of Molecular Biology', *Minerva*, vol. 10, pp. 51—82.

Mullins, N. C. *et al.* (1977) 'The Group Structure of Co-Citation Clusters: a Comparative Study', *American Sociological Review*, vol. 42, pp. 552—62.

Pannekoek, A. (1953) 'The Discovery of Neptune', *Centaurus*, vol. 3, pp. 126—37.

Pearce Williams, L. (1970) 'Normal Science, Scientific Revolutions and the History of Science', in *Criticism and the Growth of Knowledge*, ed. Lakatos and Musgrave (1970) pp. 49—50.

Pearce Williams, L. (1980) 'The Essential Thomas Kuhn', *History of Science*, vol. 18, pp. 68—74.

Phillips, D. L. (1977) *Wittgenstein and Scientific Knowledge*, London, Macmillan.

Pickering, A. (1981) 'The Role of Interests in High-Energy Physics: the Choice Between Charm and Colour', *Sociology of the Sciences Yearbook*, vol. 5, pp. 107—38.

Pickering, A. (forthcoming) 'The Hunting of the Quark', *Isis*.

Popper, K. (1970) 'Normal Science and its Dangers', in *Criticism and the Growth of Knowledge*, ed. Lakatos and Musgrave (1970) pp. 51—8.

Putnam, H. (1975) *Collected Papers*, vol. 2, Cambridge University Press.

Quine, W. V. O. (1953) 'Two Dogmas of Empiricism', in *From a Logical Point of View*, Harvard University Press.

Scheffler, I. (1967) *Science and Subjectivity*, New York, Bobbs-Merrill.

Shapin, S. (1979) 'The Politics of Observation, Cerebral Anatomy and Social Interests in the Edinburgh Phrenology Disputes', *Sociological Review Monograph*, no. 27, pp. 139—78.

Shapin, S. (1980) 'Social Uses of Science 1660—1800', in *The Ferment of Knowledge: Changing Perspectives of Eighteenth-Century Science*, ed. R. S. Porter and G. S. Rousseau, Cambridge University Press.

Shapin, S. (forthcoming) 'The Moral Force of Nature', Edinburgh University Press.

Stegmüller, W. (1976) *The Structure and Dynamics of Theories*, New York, Springer.

Teich, M. and Young, R. M. (eds) (1973) *Changing Perspectives in the History of Science*, London, Heinemann.

Thackray, A. (1970) 'Science: Has its Present Past a Future', in *Historical and Philosophical Perspectives of Science*, ed. R. H. Stuewer, Minnesota University Press.

Thackray, A. (1974) 'Natural Knowledge in Cultural Context', *American History Review*, vol. 74, pp. 672—709.

Truesdell, C. (1967) 'Reactions of late Baroque Mechanics to Success, Conjecture, Error, and Failure in Newton's *Principia*', *Texas Quarterly*, vol. 10, pp. 238—58.

Wallis, R. (ed.) (1979) 'On the Margins of Science', *Sociological Review Monograph*, no. 27, Keele at the University Press.

Watkins, J. (1970) 'Against "Normal Science"', in *Criticism and the Growth of Knowledge*, ed. Lakatos and Musgrave (1970) pp. 25—37.

Wieder, D. L. (1976) *Language and Social Reality*, The Hague, Mouton.

Winsor, M. P. (1976) *Starfish, Jellyfish, and the Order of Life*, Yale University Press.

Wittgenstein, L. (1953) *Philosophical Investigations*, Oxford, Blackwell.

Wittgenstein, L. (1964) *Remarks on the Foundations of Mathematics*, Oxford, Blackwell.

Woolgar, S. W. (1976) 'Writing on Intellectual History of Scientific Development: the Use of Discovery Accounts', *Social Studies of Science*, vol. 6, pp. 395—422.

Wynne, B. (1976) 'C. G. Barkla and the *J* Phenomenon', *Social Studies of Science*, vol. 6, nos 3 and 4, pp. 307—47.

Wynne, B. (1979) 'Physics and Psychics: Science, Symbolic Action and Social Control in Late Victorian England', in *Natural Order*, ed. Barnes and Shapin (1979).

Young, R. M. (1969) 'Malthus and the Evolutionists', *Past and Present*, vol. 43, pp. 109—45.

Young, R. M. (1973) 'The Historiographic and Ideological Contexts of the Nineteenth-Century Debate on Man's Place in Nature', in *Changing Perspectives in the History of Science*, ed. Teich and Young (1973).

Index

NOTE: book titles appear in *italics*, and **boldface** is used for pages primarily on indexed headings